BLESSED
ISLE

One Man's Ireland

John Seymour

BLESSED ISLE

One Man's Ireland

COLLINS & BROWN

First published in Great Britain in 1992
by Collins & Brown Limited
Mercury House
195 Knightsbridge
London SW7 1RE

British Library Cataloguing-in-Publication Data.
A catalogue record for this book
is available from the British Library

ISBN 1 85585 054 0 (hardback)
ISBN 1 85585 114 8 (paperback)

Conceived, edited and designed by Collins & Brown Limited
Editorial Director: Gabrielle Townsend
Editor: Sarah Bloxham
Researcher: Angela Ashe
Designed by: Ruth Hope

Phototypeset by Falcon Graphic Art Ltd,
Wallington, Surrey
Printed and bound in Great Britain
by The Bath Press

Contents

I dedicate this book to Angela Ashe, my fellow adventurer, without whose tireless practical help, and invaluable critical judgement the book could never have been written.

Foreword

~

WELL, I THINK I MUST APOLOGIZE to nearly everybody: to the English, for the nasty things I have said about Henry VIII; to the Irish, because I have found so very few blemishes in their beautiful country (but you mustn't find any of course); to the Catholics, because I have occasionally been slightly snide perhaps about the Hierarchy; to the Protestants, because I have said nice things about the Catholics; to the Puritans, because I have said what I think about Oliver Cromwell; to the people of Ulster, because I have not even mentioned their superbly beautiful country; to my neighbours, because I have chatted about them without their leave; and probably to a hundred other parties and people, for all kinds of diverse reasons. I am seriously thinking of buying a one-way ticket to South America, and if I had any money, which I have not, I would even now be salting it away in an Argentinian bank.

I started writing this book with the most innocent and disingenuous of intentions: merely to report what it was like, first to visit this country, and then to come and live here. I just wanted it to be a simple personal account. I was fully determined to keep as far away from history — and even more certainly from politics — as I possibly could. Which side do I take about the present squabbles in Northern Ireland? Well I don't take any, so that's that.

But then I found that you cannot even poke your nose into this country without getting it rubbed in history, in politics, in religion, the lot. History cries out from every bush and hedgerow, from every one of the hundreds of ruined castles, abbeys, and Celtic Christian cells and crosses littered about, from the deserted barracks and forts, the great crumbling Georgian mansions and the ghost-haunted ruins of long-gone hamlets and villages, and from the reminiscences of one's friends, neighbours and acquaintances. And you cannot hear about, or read about, Irish history without finding views that are biased in one way or another. If anyone wrote an impartial history of Ireland it would probably be as boring as hell and the writer would bring

7

upon himself the execration of everyone. Besides, could you ever expect an impartial history of the United States by one of the survivors of the Battle of Wounded Knee?

I must have read every history of Ireland I could lay my hands on. What makes them so compulsively readable is that none of them is impartial. This book is no doubt as partial as any of them, but it is most emphatically not a history book. It is a book of personal observations and reminiscences, and if it does not annoy you in some way or other then all I can say is: I am most surprised!

South America here I come!

John Seymour
County Wexford, 1991

PART ONE

FIRST IMPRESSIONS

CHAPTER ONE

〜

The Night Voyage

THE FARM THAT I USED TO INHABIT in Pembrokeshire, in West Wales, lay at the foot of a little mountain called Carn Ingli. Occasionally I used to climb this little mountain, which, although only just over a thousand feet, looked like a real mountain, and I would sit on the rock on top of it and gaze about me. Sometimes I would climb at night, sometimes by day. Sometimes I would climb it drunk, sometimes sober. If I was drunk when I started climbing it I was sober by the time I got down again. A Celtic saint named Saint Brynach once lived two miles from my farm, where he built his church at a place called Nevern. He used to sit on top of Carn Ingli too and it is said that the angels used to feed him there. They never fed me but then I am not a saint.

One day when I climbed it, during the day and sober, I noticed that the air was extraordinarily clear. When I turned round on the climb up and looked behind me I saw my own farm looking so close that I felt I could touch it: I could count every one of my sheep and every one of my cows. When I looked further away I could see every sharp clear detail of the landscape as far as the horizon. When I got to the top I looked around the great sweep of Cardigan Bay and could see the mountains of Snowdonia as clearly as if they were a mile away.

I then turned round and looked west — and it was that one fateful vision that altered the whole course of my life. I could see the sharp little mounts that rise up from the plain near Saint Davids of course, and the blue sea beyond. I could see the islands of Ramsey and Skomer and Skokholm as sharp as needles. But what changed my life was that, over the bright blue brilliance that was the sea — and it merged with the sky so that there was no horizon — I could just discern a sight which stopped my very breath and seemed to turn my heart upside down: hills, hills, a range of hills, so faint as to be like a mirage, apparently hanging in the sky. It was so unexpected. I had looked over that sea a hundred times before and seen no hills. I gazed and gazed, for an hour perhaps, and if I had been sober when I climbed the mountain I was drunk when I came down.

After that it was inevitable that I should go in search of those hills. I do not believe that anyone with more sensitivity than an ape could see them and not wish to go to them. I like to think that Saint Patrick saw the same sight before he crossed the Irish Sea. I crossed it probably in greater comfort than he did (we are told that he was taken across as a slave) because I went on the Fishguard-Rosslare ferry. In those days she was a fine solidly-built old motor-ship and there was even a bunk-room for such as wanted to sleep away the voyage over.

I sailed at three in the morning, but did not avail myself of the bunk-room because I found more lively company in the bar. The saloon was packed, mostly with working-class Irishmen who had been working in England. There was a scattering of women and a few lively children who did not seem to be the least bit worried about being awake in the small hours of the morning. They all sat clustered around the round tables, and as the night wore on these tables became covered with glasses and bottles. As for me, I leant against the bar at first, drinking an unaccustomed drink: draught Guinness, which I had always understood was the 'wine' of the country to which I was going. I must say I knocked back the dark stuff aboard that ferry boat with some enthusiasm. I felt that I must get into the right spirit for my new adventure, and anyway, it is quite a nice drink.

Meanwhile, I got into conversation with a man who came up to buy a round for himself and his friends and he asked me what I did. When I told him I was a farmer, and withal a small farmer, he told me he had been one too, and we became friends. He invited me to go back to the table at which he sat, and soon I found myself totally absorbed into a most lively crowd. I had met many individual Irish people on my travels, notably in the colonial service before the Second World War, and as fellow officers in the King's African Rifles in which regiment I had served out that conflict, and I had always found something particularly likeable about them. Most of them had been middle-class or professional-class individuals, but these people aboard the ferry were working-class and there were a lot of them. I found them immediately ready to be friendly with me. One middle-aged motherly lady drew a locket out of her bag and told me she had just got it from Lourdes, where she had been on pilgrimage. It had been blessed by a cardinal. I admired it, wondering what I was supposed to make of it, and gave it back; whereupon she passed it round to the other members of the company who did know what to do with it. They each kissed it reverently and crossed themselves with it, before handing it on. The owner gave me a self-deprecating smile and said, 'Of course you know we're very superstitious.' I told her I didn't think she was superstitious at all, I was just ignorant.

They were interested in me, although a great natural courtesy forbade them from asking probing questions. They were interested in Wales, and the Welsh, about whom they knew nothing. They knew far more about England (more than I did, many of them), but Wales was a closed book to them: it was just somewhere that you travelled over, generally at night, in a train, after having got off, or being about to get aboard, a ship.

Seventeen years of farming in Welsh-speaking Wales had given me a true respect for the Welsh people. These years had made me very aware that Wales is a separate nation, not just some carbuncle on the side of England. The Welsh are great talkers. They have a very serious, almost sombre, side to their natures but they can be very witty too. But these people I was with, their conversation was all repartee. Their wit flashed like summer lightning and it was hard for a stolid Englishman to keep up with it.

But talk soon gave way to song. Over the other side of the saloon a woman struck up, in a hauntingly beautiful voice, 'The Wild Colonial Boy'. The moment she sang the first note a hush fell over the rest of us. I reflected that if she had started singing in an English pub nobody would have stopped talking to listen to her and probably someone would have got up and turned the juke box on.

When she finished there was loud applause. Then a young man at our table pulled out a tin whistle (what we used to call a penny whistle when I was a boy) and he got such a lively jig out of this cheap and simple instrument that it was almost impossible to resist leaping up and dancing.

Then a man sang, then a young girl. They did not sing the hackneyed Irish-American songs that English people imagine Irish people sing but fine folk songs, many of them certainly very old (dated by the historical events they recorded). Some were nostalgic songs about beautiful countryside particularly dear to the person who had composed the song and a simple and satisfying lifestyle long since abandoned, but many of the songs that were sung that night were about real men and women, girls and boys: not abstractions of people but real people, with names to them, people who had once lived,

13

and died, or fallen in love, or had adventures. For folk songs the world over are about actual people — which is what makes them different from city songs which are all about abstractions.

One thing I quickly discovered that night is that if a man or a woman, or a child for that matter (because several very young ones, urged by their elders, got up unselfconsciously to sing), began a song, he or she knew that song right through to the end. Once when an old man faltered there were encouraging cries of 'Keep right on there! Don't give up! Don't give up!' And he didn't give up, but kept right on to the end.

But generally the singers were never interrupted, except with the occasional beautifully-timed interjection, such as 'Good girl there! Good singer! Good singer!' And if anybody in the saloon did forget themselves so much as to start to chatter there would be immediate shushing, and: 'Give the man order there! Give order! Give the singer a chance!' And the offender would quickly discover that what he had started to say was not so very important after all.

Another thing I discovered was that nearly everyone in that large company knew at least one song and, sometimes first playing hard to get, would sing it. And the worse the singer was (and we were not all nightingales) the louder would be the shouts of encouragement and the warmer the praise at the end! Even I, who must have been a bit of a puzzle to them, was made to sing. I gave them 'The Gloucestershire Shepherd's Song' and the warmth of their applause was a measure of the atrociousness of my singing. But to paraphrase Doctor Johnson, an Englishman who can sing is like a dog that can dance on its hind legs: what is remarkable is not that he does it well but that he does it at all.

Being so used to Welsh singing, which still echoed in those days in the valleys around my farm, I was used to choral singing, where if one person began a song (nearly always in Welsh of course) everybody else would join in, each person singing a different part so that the song would become a great swelling harmony. But these people sang solos. Their music was melodic, not harmonic.

A mouth organ struck up, with the whistle and an instrument I had never seen before: a small drum made out of the rim of a corn sieve (I was told) with the skin of a young goat (or preferably a greyhound — particularly if it had been a good running dog) stretched over it called a *bodhrán*. This made a rather barbaric sound when struck: it gave to the music a sort of wildness that I found exciting.

14

I formed the conclusion, and I now know that it was the correct one, that these were just ordinary Irish working people going back for a holiday from their work of 'Building England up and pulling England down' as one of the songs they sang has it, back to little scattered cottages and cabins mostly in the west.

This was twenty years ago, when the people still held very firmly to their ancient folk culture. You would not readily get such a night voyage aboard the Fishguard ferry today. And yet the last time I came over, just before Christmas in 1988, the singers and the musicians were in the ascendancy and a couple of score of people sang and played the whole voyage across, turning what might have been a most tedious vigil into a delight. In the summer though they could never do it. There are too many tourists then, and generally some tuneless fellow with a guitar.

Stirred by the music, I went up on deck to find that dawn was just about to break, and the light of the Tuskar lighthouse was flashing away on our port bow. Ahead, far far away, I could just see the blue outline of those magical mountains, the mirage of which had lured me to come over in the first place.

Whether it was the sight of these mountains, or the splendid dawn over the sea, or the wild music that was still ringing in my ears — or all those pints of Guinness I had drunk (and so few of which I had paid for because my friends below had been persistently generous) — I do not know, but I knew that I was going to love this country I was going to. I had fallen head over heels in love with it before I had even set foot upon it.

CHAPTER TWO

～

The Open Road

WHEN I DID SET FOOT ON LAND though some slight disenchantment set in. All my new-found friends vanished into the morning as though they had never existed and I never saw one of them again. And there I was, stranded all alone on Rosslare quay, at eight o'clock in the morning, without very much idea of what I was going to do next.

At the end of the quay was a canteen with a bar in it. Inside a few sleepy dock workers were trying to liven themselves up with whiskey. It didn't seem to be working. Me, I had a mug of tea or two. The effect of the Guinness, the euphoria of all that music, and good company, and the splendid dawning, were fast wearing off. I felt I could do with a couple of hours' sleep, but that was not to be.

Up on the wall I saw a small advertisement. It read: Horses for hire. I had no real idea what I was going to do. I had a small suitcase with me, with some changes of clothes and a razor. I vaguely thought of wandering westward until I got to those blue mountains. Seeing the advertisement gave me an idea: what if I hired a saddle horse and rode to the mountains?

I asked one of the dockers how far away the livery stable was. 'Five miles,' he answered, 'but *long* miles mind you!' I wondered how one mile could be longer than another but then I had only been in Ireland for half an hour. I set out to walk to the livery stable, carrying my little suitcase. The country was flat and dull, and very sandy. The few trees that there were looked windswept, the land poor.

The five miles were, indeed, long ones. But I came to a substantial farmstead at last, with stables and loose boxes, and was greeted by a strong stocky man. He asked me into his house and gave me some coffee and we discussed many things before we discussed the matter of horse hiring. The man's name was Billy Rackard and he told me that he had been an athlete before he had taken to owning horses. I didn't know it then but I found out later that I was talking to one of the most famous men in Ireland (at least, I have never met an Irishman who has not heard of the Rackard brothers). They had been players of hurley, a kind of aerial hockey that the Irish play, and it was said that they had been the supreme players of all time at this game. Now, he has had another change of career. I was walking along the quay at Wexford, a week ago before I wrote this. I heard my name called by a man standing outside a furniture shop. I thought I vaguely recognized him but then I spotted the name over the store: *Rackard's Furniture Store.* 'Gave up the horses,' he said, 'and I run this instead.'

But back to my first visit: No, he would not hire me a saddle horse, but yes, he would charter me a cob, named Dolly, and a governess car. Now a governess car is not the most dashing of conveyances. I would rather have had a smart trap, or sulky, or spider, and a high-stepping hackney to pull it. I once drove from the North Foreland in Kent to Cornwall in a governess car and it was a slow old job. But as Billy Rackard would let me have nothing else, a governess car it had to be.

'Ye'll be having a drop before you go,' he said. A 'drop', as I discovered then and have known ever since is not a drop at all but about four fingers of Irish whiskey. Well, after having another 'drop', because a bird never flew on one wing, I clambered up into the governess car, took up the reins, and rattled off.

Dolly went along at a fairly tireless trot. The country was still flat, cut up into small fields by high hedges, which the Irish call ditches, and well farmed. It reminded me of my own country, East Anglia, before the agribusinessmen had slaughtered all the hedges and most of the trees.

The population was obviously very sparse. There was the occasional smallish farmhouse, which had obviously once been part of a big estate, quite comely and well-built, originally a typical tenanted yeoman farmstead. There was a scattering of new bungalows, boring and featureless and having no affinity with the countryside in which they stood. (They would have been more at home in Texas.) There were many small cabins: tiny, single-storey one-roomed or two-roomed dwellings, a few still with thatched roofs but most roofed with corrugated iron. Some of these cabins were inhabited — mostly by very old people. Many were empty and falling down. Since that time most of them have fallen down completely. And there were mansions. Dolly would clip-clop along the road past a great stone wall, built to enclose a well-wooded park, and occasionally one could get a glimpse inside of a fine country house, very often a Georgian stone-built mansion, which I knew from my reading had probably been built by the descendants of Oliver Cromwell's conquering soldiers.

When you drive a horse and cart it is very easy to stop and talk to people, and I got talking to an oldish man who was standing by the gate of his bungalow.

'Do you know of anyone who would put the horse and me up for the night?' I asked. Truth to tell, I was beginning to think it would be nice to have a comfortable night's sleep. I had had a halt at midday, and a pint of Guinness in a village pub, which doubled as a grocer's shop, and doubled again as an undertaker, and I had picketed Dolly out for a couple of hours on some good clovery grass by the roadside and had a short snooze myself, but I was beginning to think about clean sheets and blankets.

'I'll ask herself if she'd let ye sleep in the spare room,' he said. Herself said yes. Himself said he'd peg the horse out in his back garden. 'I was a great horseman meself when I was younger!' he told me.

Together we unharnessed Dolly and rubbed her down with straw and gave her some of the crushed oats I had in the cart, and then my host tied her to a 14-pound weight he had in the back garden.

'That horse will drag that weight and get at your cabbages,' I told him.

'No she will not. And sure if she does she's welcome to 'em. It's grand to see a horse. Very few of 'em about in these days.'

So we went in and had a great supper, sat talking for a couple of hours, and then I fell into bed. In the morning I was appalled to see that Dolly *had* dragged her anchor, and had eaten every one of my kind hosts' cabbages, stalks and all. But the two of them roared with laughter about it. They seemed to think it the greatest joke in the world. If they had been my cabbages I should have been bloody furious!

As Dolly and I clattered off again, I gave a small boy a lift. He was one of the race of Tinkers, now called Itinerants or Travellers. I had met many of these people in England and Wales, in company with Gypsies (people of true Romany stock) among whom I had had many friends. There is rivalry between the two races of people (and they are, racially, quite distinct) for the Tinkers, when they come to Britain, tend to behave in ways that the *gaujo* (non-Gypsy) considers anti-social and the Romany Gypsies get blamed for it.

Not at all anti-social, my little hitchhiker was an engaging, red-headed

boy, about ten years old, and we chatted about this or that. (I was completely fascinated by the way he spoke English.) But he very soon got down
to business, the real reason for our conversation. He wanted, no more nor
less, to buy the horse and cart from me.

'I'll be givin' ye thirty pounds,' he said.

'Have you got it?' I asked.

'Sure an' I've got it. More'n that too.'

'Well I'm afraid it belongs to another man.'

'I'll make it forty — wi' the car.'

'But it's not mine to sell.'

'Oh — when ye're after sellin' it you never need see the other man at all.'

Both the morals and the economics of this proposition seemed questionable, so I politely refused the deal. I delivered the boy to his home —
an encampment of wild-looking people living in horse-drawn *vardos* or basic
broken-down trailer-caravans — and went on my way. I headed vaguely
westward, still with some idea of reaching those mystic mountains. I never
got there. It is now more than twenty years since I first saw the vision of
them, from the top of Carn Ingli, and I still haven't got there. I will though
— always, as we say in Ireland, please God.

I did get to the foot of them once, about five years ago. In Wales, I had
been a passenger in a car that had hit a bank and rolled over, badly injuring
both of my hands. There were various visits to hospitals, and x-rayings, and
I began to realize that conventional medical science, although it may be able
to give you a heart transplant, or take bits out of your brain, knows nothing
about the mechanics of bones. I was bewailing this fact to Richie Roche, who
keeps a pub in New Ross. He poured out five fingers of whiskey and said,
'Swallow that. You'll need it!'

Wonderingly, I swallowed it. Then he said, 'Come on — jump in my
car.' I jumped in. We drove north. After quite a long time we stopped at
a pub where I was prescribed another five fingers of whiskey: to reinforce
the first five. Then we turned off the main road and went eastward, towards
the mystic mountains. We drove right to the foot of them: it was as close
as I have so far got to them.

We came to a big farmhouse. In the yard outside were perhaps twenty
cars. We entered the house and turned into a large room, which had on its
walls a photograph of the Pope, a print of a painting of the Holy Virgin,
and a notice which read: *No Animals on Saturdays*. Today was a Saturday.

I took the last space on the benches that surrounded the room. After a short silence people began to talk again and the talk was all about various bones out of joint: bad backs, dislocated hips, bulls' stifle joints, stallions' fetlocks and all the rest of it.

From time to time a huge man in white overalls would lean in through the door, look around the company like the Captain of the Guillotine picking out his next aristocrat, and crook his finger at one trembling victim. As the chosen one got up and tottered out, a deathly silence would descend on the rest of us. The silence would be broken by a loud yell from the next room. As I sat there waiting for my turn I found that the effects of Richie's whiskey were beginning to wear off.

My turn came. In I went. The huge man took my left hand, looked at it, and contemptuously threw it away. 'Thumb's broke,' he said. 'Can't do nothin' wit that!'

The next thing I knew was an excruciating pain in my right forefinger. My God, I thought, he's pulled it off! While I was looking to see if he had dropped it on the floor, the same thing happened to the next finger, and the next. And I knew immediately that he had cured them. Before, I could not move them at all, now I could. They have been perfect ever since.

'What do I — er — owe you?' I asked.

'Whatever ye like.'

I gave him a tenner. Afterwards I learnt that a fiver was the going rate. Bulls' stifle joints, of course, were more.

But all this happened years after my travels with Dolly and the governess car, so I have not so much jumped in my story as taken a quantum leap.

CHAPTER THREE

~

The Great Fort

FTER MANY MEANDERINGS and various adventures, Dolly and I arrived at a place where our further progress west was barred by a huge estuary.

I had arrived at the village of Duncannon. It was a fine, compact village, much more like a 'proper' village than the scattered collections of little houses and bungalows we had so far seen. It had a big church on a hill with a fine view overlooking the estuary, and the one main street leading down to the water had what were obviously fishermen's cottages on both sides of it. At the bottom of this street was a three-storey hotel. I went inside.

'Have you got a room?' I asked.

'Sure and we have.'

'And — er — could you put a horse up?'

'Sure and we could. There's a stable at the back. We can put your cart in the shelter too.'

So I stabled Dolly, brushed her down and fed her, and the landlord of the hotel brought in a bale of hay. No horse, I gathered, had graced that stable for many a year. The horse age was over in Ireland.

I put my bag in my room and went for a stroll. Over the road from the hotel was a wide sandy beach, several miles long. To the right was the estuary, miles wide, with hills on the far bank, the sea perhaps five miles to the south. This was Waterford Harbour, I knew from the map. I wandered along the great beach. Facing the bay, I could see, if I looked to my right, a rocky headland jutting out into the water and on it a mighty fort, the guns of which could have commanded the approaches to the two rivers which I knew debouched into Waterford Harbour (one, the Suir, allowed ships to get to Waterford itself, and the other, the Barrow, led the way to New Ross).

21

I had absolutely no idea then that the Barrow would one day be *my* river and that I would spend a sizeable chunk of my life on her banks. To my left I could see the flashing of a lighthouse, and this I knew was the Hook, a great spit of rock which springs from the east side of the mouth of the bay and partly cuts it off.

I strolled back and, passing a small pub which was just over the road from my hotel, heard the sound of singing. In I went. There I beheld perhaps a dozen sailors (not fishermen but matelots from the Irish Navy), one soldier, and one fine-looking man with a big red beard. This man, I found, was the caretaker of the great fort, which belonged to the Irish War Department. The sailors had come from Cork to form a guard of honour at the statue of John Barry, the founder of the United States Navy, who was a Wexford man and whose statue stands on the waterfront of that town; next day was his anniversary, and the soldier was the driver of the lorry in which they were going to travel. They were all drinking stout or whiskey and singing rebel songs.

I was absorbed into their company immediately, as if they had known me all their lives. The red-bearded man bought me a drink and told me his name was Paddy Burke. 'I'm one of Strongbow's Normans,' he said. 'Burke's a Norman name. There's lots of Normans round here. He landed at Baginbun — you must have passed it in yer pony and car.'

I had indeed gone quite near it. A force of Normans, having sailed from Pembrokeshire, landed there on 1 May 1169 and cut off the promontory with a big bank and ditch. They had already allied themselves with one of the Irish chieftains who was at war with the others, and so they quickly conquered the whole country. I have a friend who lives in a great castle right in the middle of Ireland and he has an ingenious explanation of what happened next:

'The Normans swaggered about with their armour and their helmets and their great plumes, feeling terribly pleased with themselves, but the native musicians, with their rude fiddles or tin whistles or whatever the hell they had, sat down in front of them and played: a-diddle-de-dee-a-diddle-de-dee. And those mighty warriors were so seduced by the music that when the natives paraded their prettiest young maidens before them, they married these instead of returning to their stern warrior wives back in Normandy. They went native and forgot all their silly martial ideas and became like everybody else.'

It's a pity, I thought, that Cromwell's warriors were not also seduced by a-diddle-de-dee-a-diddle-de-dee, but they marched to a far more military drum.

I have a theory that the Irish actually seduced those early invaders by making them laugh; you can't go on being a conquering hero when you are splitting your sides with laughter all the time. But to have made one of Cromwell's Ironsides laugh would have been too much even for Irish wit.

Back in the pub, the rebel songs were stirring. They were not songs about the present troubles in Northern Ireland but about heroic rebellions of long ago. Many of the best of them were about the uprising of Wexford peasants in 1798. I joined right lustily in the choruses. But I noticed that the one soldier present, whose name was Murphy, was eyeing me with some surprise. 'But ye're an Englishman,' he said. 'How can you be likin' such songs as that?'

'Look I wasn't alive in 1798,' I said. 'Therefore I wasn't on one side or the other. In any case, the war you're singing about wasn't a war between the English and the Irish. It was a war between the Irish country people and the English government. And that government was busy at the time oppressing the English country people too.'

And so we went on singing and boasting, like sailors and soldiers do, and ribbing each other, and then, lo, it was chucking-out time — several hours after it really. And then it was that I found myself forming part of a human chain, from which I could not escape. I was trapped. I had somehow come to be in the middle of a long line of men, each man linked to the next by a crate of bottled Guinness. I could not escape from the line without dropping my ends of two of them, with shattering results.

We filed right past my hotel. I cast a longing eye up to the window of the room in which I had hoped to sleep that night. We filed along the road until, very shortly, we came to the massive ramparts and huge iron gates of the great fort itself. Paddy Burke unlocked the gates and in we all filed. When we were in he slammed the gates shut behind us and turned the lock. We then filed into a cavernous chamber with a vaulted roof and a great open peat fire at the end. There were army tables and army chairs about. We applied ourselves with marvellous application to the beer. 'If we are to finish all this tonight,' I said, 'it'll be a shaky guard of honour in the morning!'

'Och the boys'll manage to stay upright please God,' said the petty officer in command.

'You're sitting in the very place,' Paddy Burke told me, 'where the croppy boys used to be sentenced to be hanged.'

The sailors had just been singing a sad song called 'The Croppy Boy', about one of the thousands of young Wexford boys and men who were rounded up after the failure of the '98 rebellion and shot or hanged. Duncannon Fort was the one place in the county that held out against the insurgents of '98, and was afterwards used as the place of confinement and trial of most of them, on account of its commodious dungeons, before they were shipped across to the Geneva Barracks to be hanged. The government's soldiers had a merry habit of dipping their prisoners' heads in boiling pitch while they were waiting to be sentenced. When the 'pitch cap' came off, their hair and scalp came off with it, hence the term 'croppy boy'. Or they might put a pitch-soaked cap of canvas on the victim's head and set fire to it. I seem to have jumped into Irish history at the deep end, I thought.

Suddenly the door was flung open with a bang, and a sailor came in bearing a huge dish of smoking pigs' trotters, called *crúibíní* in Irish. He dumped them on the table and we all fell to. They were magnificent: the perfect dish for sailors and soldiers, and ex-soldiers, after a long night of singing songs, arguing and drinking Guinness. I went outside and stood on the ramparts built to the orders of Queen Elizabeth, and the moon had risen and was glinting over the bay, and the Hook Lighthouse flashed away to the south, and it was very beautiful.

I did not sleep in my hotel bedroom that night. I slept what was left of it in the house of Paddy Burke, which was one of the more modern buildings (I would guess c.1918) that had been built round the perimeter of the fort. Paddy and his charming wife Phyllis had five young girls and three young boys, and when I came down for breakfast in the morning they were all over the place, splashing their faces in the sink, brushing their hair, pulling their socks on — and a lively, lovely lot they were too.

When the time came for me to move on, driving first past the strange, lonely and lost headland of Baginbun, where the Norman raiders had settled, my mind was drawn back to Pembrokeshire, in West Wales, from whence those Normans had invaded and where I had lived for the past seventeen years. A mile from the little farm I had in Pembrokeshire is the hamlet of Nevern, which has a magnificent Norman church and a beautiful little river from which my friends and neighbours used to gaff, illegally, salmon. Behind the church is a hill, much overgrown with scrubby woodland. On top of it, unregarded by the tourists who flock to see the church below with its ogham stone and famous Celtic cross, are the ruinous foundations of a castle, once the home of Prince Rhys ap Tewdewr whose daughter Nesta played an important part in the Welsh settlement of Ireland.

It is therefore easy to see why those first invaders succumbed so rapidly and completely to the seductions of Ireland's music, language, culture, and pretty young girls, because they were, nearly all of them, half-Celtic already, the leaders all sharing one common Welsh ancestor, the beautiful Nesta, the so-called Helen of Wales. Her father, Rhys ap Tewdewr, tried to defend his princedom of South Wales against Henry I but was, alas, beaten. Henry took his beautiful daughter as a hostage and looked after her so well that he begat a son by her. (Two of the first of the Norman invaders of Ireland were Meiler and Robert FitzHenry, the grandchildren of King Henry and Nesta.)

Nesta was eventually released by Henry I and married Gerald de Windsor, constable of Pembroke Castle. By him she had three sons, who all went by the name of FitzGerald, and also a daughter, called by the beautiful Welsh name of Angharat, who married William de Barri of Manorbier, in Pembrokeshire. William and Angharat had three sons too, who all had a part in the invasion of Ireland. One was the famous chronicler Giraldus Cambrensis (or Gerald the Welshman) and he wrote a marvellous account of the Norman invasion.

Now the beautiful Nesta seemed to have a penchant for constables of Norman castles, for she either married or was mistress of another one: Stephen, Constable of Cardigan. And that marriage produced yet another of the invaders of Ireland: Robert FitzStephen.

So it would not be far wrong to say that Ireland was conquered and subsequently divided up between the descendants of one woman. Within a couple of generations the invaders had become settlers; they had forgotten Norman-French (English they had never known), learnt to think and speak in Irish, and had adopted all the customs of the country. But I myself could not 'go native' and had got to get back to the land of Nesta. I had not yet seen my magic mountains — but I knew I would return.

Commissioned by the BBC to record some radio programmes on Ireland, I did return, in 1960, and swopping Dolly for a motorcar I pressed on north, right up to County Donegal. But no holiday can last for ever, and I had a farm to get back to. My Irish idyll had come to an end, for now at least.

PART TWO

SETTLING IN

CHAPTER FOUR

~

We Move to Ireland

BACK ON MY FARM I slogged away for ten or twelve years, farming and teaching young people from all over the world to become self-sufficient. My marriage broke up; my children grew up and got married and started having children of their own. They wanted to take over the farm, and I had begun to find that writing was now my first love. Once more I caught a glimpse of those magic mountains glinting over the sea, and when a friend, James Wharram, a designer of twin-hulled yachts, asked me to go over and see his cottage in Ireland I agreed to go. It was decided that a young lady named Angela Ashe should come with us.

Angela Ashe had come to my farm for a holiday, as a friend of a friend, when she was fourteen years old, and had just stayed on. She simply became one of the family; I suppose I came to look upon her as just another one of my daughters. She began to help me more and more. I am very untidy, and I began to find that things were beginning to be tidied up — I could actually find things that I needed. I also noticed that if anybody was working usefully on the farm or in the house it was sure to be Angela. She is Irish, born in Dublin but reared in England since she was a baby. On her mother's side she is a Fitzmaurice, so one of her ancestors was almost certainly one of the Norman invaders of Ireland and a descendant of Nesta. Naturally, when James Wharram asked me to go and see his Irish cottage, I asked her if she wanted to go too.

So we set out for the Fishguard ferry, Jim Wharram, Angela and I, in my car, made the short sea voyage again, and drove west through the dark towards the town of New Ross. We left the main road and wound through country lanes bordered by big beech trees. We came to a farmyard and turned down the track that went through it, a mile-long muddy track with serious puddles in it. We stopped. It was very dark. The track was very muddy. We went through a gap in the hedge and could see a little rough stone cottage in the light of our torch. We went in, found some paraffin lamps and lit them, got some dry sticks together and lit a fire in a little broken fireplace at one end of the main room, sat around it for some time and then went upstairs. Here we found three small rooms, and we each slept on the floor of one of them. There was practically no furniture.

My room was tiny and at the south end of the house. I woke up at daylight and looked out of the window to see an absolutely breath-taking view. A great estuarial river, which I knew to be the Barrow, wound its way around the foot of the little wooded hill the cottage was on, swung round to the left and then made a noble turn round to the right to where it disappeared behind another wooded hill. This was not so much a house with a view, I thought, as a view with a house. And not much of a house I soon realized; the cottage was two-storeyed with two rooms downstairs, one of them a fair size but the other a minute, damp, concrete-walled and -floored box which I supposed had once been the dairy. Upstairs: just the plank floor, rough partition walls with crumbling plaster (we woke with our hair white from its dust), and signs of wet in various places where the roof had been leaking. It was not altogether a very encouraging sight. There was no electricity and no water.

The cottage stood in a one-acre enclosure which one could only call wilderness. Decades ago it had been a haggard, or stackyard; now it was full of tall bracken, brambles, thorn bushes and gorse. Over the lane was a long narrow field, perhaps two acres, which went with the house, and beyond this strip, which was steep, was the bank of the Barrow. At high tide the water came up to the bottom of the little cliff below the field, which had tall ash trees along the top of it; at low tide there were perhaps sixty yards of steeply sloping mud. The river was about half a mile wide and it had navigation buoys on it, for at every high tide a few small coasters steam up or down it, travelling to or from New Ross. The far bank, which was in County Kilkenny (we were in County Wexford), was a mixture of woods and well farmed land, with a scattering of farmhouses set back from the river. One cottage, rather like ours, was visible about half a mile upstream (to the right) on the opposite bank, and there was another riverside cottage a mile downstream from us on our bank. There was a stone-built quay, which must have been built for schooners or barges, and at its landward end two massive and superbly built lime kilns. I could imagine schooners coming in from South Wales, in days gone by, and unloading Welsh coal on to the quay, and barges unloading limestone, and the two substances being burnt in the kilns to make quicklime for mortar or use on the land. Now, though, it seemed the most deserted place in the world, deserted but completely magical. There was another small empty cottage right on the river, lost in great trees. I supposed this must have been occupied by an estate servant who acted as lime-burner, but heard that the last occupants were two old unmarried brothers, the Clearys, who caught salmon from the river, ploughed the little land they had with a donkey to grow potatoes for themselves, and occasionally worked for the council, on the roads, with their donkey and cart.

As for the house up the hill in which we had slept, I did not hear of any other occupant except Jim Wharram and his friends who had more or less camped in, rather than occupied, it for a couple of years. It had formerly been a 'cabin', like the other thousands of such that are scattered around Ireland: a single-storey rough stone cottage with, at most, two little rooms in it and an open fireplace at one end. In the 1920s, during the great Land Reform Movement, it had been compulsorily purchased from the Killowen Estate and handed over to the tenant of the land surrounding it. The Land Commission had added a second floor to it, an upper storey of brick on top of the ancient stone and mud-mortar walls, and stuck a tiny dairy on one end, made of precast concrete. The new owner, who had to pay a yearly repayment to the Land Commission which would ultimately secure complete ownership, was supposed to live in the cottage and thresh corn in the haggard once a year, in an effort to prevent absentee ownership. He never fulfilled either obligation. Except for one occasion, when some timber-fellers camped in the house, no-one can remember anybody living there before Jim Wharram bought it. And now he wanted to sell it to me.

Now, I did not so much have no money as I had a very large minus quantity of money. But both Angela and I decided that Killowen Cottage, for that was its name, was where we wanted to live. It did occur to me that if I could buy a cottage with no money but a huge debt I might just as well buy a mansion and be done with it. (A debt, if it is large enough, becomes your bank manager's problem, not yours.) But I liked Killowen. I fell in love with it, and so did Angela.

The little stone quay belonged to it, and I could dream of one day having a small sailing boat tied to the end of it. Huge mature beech trees surrounded the acre around the house. I examined the soil in that acre and

31

found that it was well drained and good, a kindly loam, although there were boulders in it (which we've since removed). A two-acre strip of rough pasture across the track, along the river, went with the house. We could dream of owning a horse, one day, and perhaps a couple of cows if we were willing to buy in a little hay occasionally. And if there were fish in that wide tidal river surely we could get some of them out? In any case we could always go down to the sea, for we intended to have a boat soon enough; the river widened out into Waterford Harbour about five miles downstream from us and thereafter, some six or eight miles further, was the open Atlantic. Five or six miles upriver was the town of New Ross where we could get anything we needed from the outside world, provided we had the money to pay for it (and by rowing boat if necessary, supposing we couldn't afford a car). We could certainly grow any vegetables we needed, and fruit, in the garden. As for fuel, there was a mass of driftwood along the river bank, and there were plenty of ash trees, on our land and just off it, some of which would have to be culled from time to time. We would not freeze to death.

As for neighbours, the nearest one was a mile away on the other side of the river. But we met some neighbours on our side during that first visit. James Wharram, who is splendidly eccentric, got us to walk back along the muddy lane to visit the Hunt family. The Hunts lived in a modern bungalow and farmed a fair-sized farm. There was John-Joe, Cathy, and their four children: two boys and two girls.

They asked us in and plied us with tea and sandwiches. They were especially pleased to see James for he had not been there for a year or two, and I found the whole family immediately likeable. John-Joe is a large man, always smiling (I find it hard to imagine him with any other expression), rather easy-going and relaxed and always radiating a kind of pleased contentment with life. Cathy, John-Joe's wife, is a great example to us all, a real country woman who can put her hand to anything. She is a great help to John-Joe on the farm, runs the house superbly and is an accomplished dress-maker (she made all of the children's clothes for them when they were younger). I did not know all that then of course. All I knew was that these people were more than friendly towards us.

'Have you got everything you want down there?' asked Cathy.

'Well, we've got no tea,' James said. She pulled out a packet of tea and put it on the table.

'And no sugar.' Some sugar followed. 'Or milk.'

'No shortage of that,' said Cathy, and a bottle was filled.

'And — er — we've got no bread.' Out came a loaf. 'And no butter to put on it.' And so on, and so on.

And finally, as if to cap it all: 'Cathy — have you got a bag to put it all in?'

Out came a bag. 'Why don't you ask them to carry it down to the cottage for you?' I said.

John-Joe just smiled.

We camped in the cottage for a day or two. Then we went back to Wales but I, for one, could not forget Killowen. James wanted me to buy the place from him. I explained that I had no money. 'Just go and live in it then,' he said, 'and rent it off me. Ten pounds a week.'

'Five pounds!' said Angela. And five pounds it was.

So the day came when Angela and I flung some belongings into my old car and boarded the ferry again. We would at least live in Killowen even if we could not afford to buy it.

My children were all living on my farm at that time, occupying the farmhouse and the numerous buildings I had put up for the people who came to be instructed in self-sufficiency. I just walked out of the place and, but for a few hand tools, some books, and clothes, left everything that I had accumulated in the last thirty years behind me. We crossed the sea and drove back across the width of County Wexford, down the long muddy track, and went into our new home.

We were in what can only be called a camping situation. We collected our water from a spring down by the river's edge (the river itself is salt), and had to carry it a hundred yards or so up the hill. We collected driftwood for the fire, for it was by now November and getting cold, and I attacked the wilderness behind the house with the slasher and scythe I had brought over with me. We had brought a couple of Tilley lamps, and there were one or two wick lamps already there, so every day there was the ritual of lamp-cleaning, filling, wick-trimming and all the rest of it.

Down by the shore amongst the bullrushes we discovered a little clinker-built pram dinghy which we named 'Moses'. The boat opened up a new world to us: the world of the river; the world of the mud flats; the saltings, which were covered only at high spring tides; the little streams and creeks that flowed into the Barrow. We would row to New Ross — in two hours if the tide was coming in — do our shopping, and then wait for as long as it took for the tide to start ebbing again so that it would take us only two hours to row home.

Back on dry land, John-Joe Hunt's brother-in-law came in with a large tractor and ploughed the acre behind the house. He struck many boulders, but was able to lift out most of them and shove them into the hedge. When he had done this I bought a little garden Rotovator, and I rotovated that land half a dozen times. Several of our neighbours took a great interest in these proceedings.

'What are you going to do with it?' asked Jimmy Foley, the owner of a small farm up on the side of a little mountain called Slieve Coilta.

'Bit of it I'm going to turn into a vegetable garden. The rest plant with wheat.'

'Wheat? But how will you be sowing it?'

'By hand. Broadcast it.'

'But those days are over, gone. You can't do that.'

'Well, I can.'

'Look, we'll come down and help you widen the gate so we can get a seed drill in. My brother-in-law Dick's got a small combine drill. We'll shove some fertilizer down the spout with the seed.'

And other neighbours drifted along, came in and looked at our field, and made the same sort of comments. I felt that they had a real resentment at the idea of us broadcasting seed by hand. But when Jimmy Foley came down to see us again the field was sown. I had broadcast it by hand, and raked it well — some three quarters of an acre of it — with a hand rake. I had also broadcast grass and clover seed in with it, for I intended to establish a grass field.

The wheat came up, thick and even. It looked superb. Then came the inevitable question: 'How are you going to reap it?'

'With a scythe.'

'You can't. We won't let you. We'll bring a combine in.'

'It's very nice of you, but I'll mow it with a scythe.'

'Look John, those days are after being over!'

Well, I did mow it with a scythe: half a day's glorious work, and I enjoyed every minute of it. Angela came along behind and bound the wheat into sheaves, tying them with their own straw in the time-honoured way. After a week or two in the shooks we built two high and noble mows, conical stacks of hay perhaps twelve foot high. The wheat would be safe from the weather there, at least until the winter gales came in, and the grain would dry and mature, held safely in the ears of the straw.

The neighbours could not get over it. 'How are you going to thresh it?' was the next question.

'In that shed there — over the back of a chair.'

'Never! We can't allow it. We'll put it through a combine for ye. Look John, it won't cost ye nothing.'

I politely declined, and went into the house for a drink.

A few weeks later, late one evening, Jimmy Foley paid us a visit, and we sat around the fire for a while chatting about this and that. 'I must be going,' said Jim. I accompanied him out of the house, we walked round the back, and — horror! — my two fine mows of wheat were gone. They had vanished as though they had never been. And in their place was Jim Foley's brother-in-law's tractor and trailer piled high with sheaves of wheat. Two of Jimmy's nephews, fine lads of sixteen years or so, were busy lashing the load down with ropes.

'Sorry John. We all talked about it, do you see. We couldn't let ye do it. Those days are over you see. We couldn't bear to think of ye bashing them sheaves over the back of a chair. So we'll run 'em through Dick's combine for ye.' And off they went into the night.

Next day they brought back the grain, many sacks of it, and for a couple of years we ate our own bread, made from our own wheat. We had a little hand-turned mill that we had brought over from Wales and this was adequate to grind what we needed in the way of flour.

I reflected upon this whole episode, and I realized, of course, that the transition from peasant farming to modern mechanized farming was still too recent for my neighbours. They felt they had left something old and bad and laborious behind them and they did not want to be reminded of the days when they, and their fathers, had to sow seed by hand and reap with a scythe or sickle. I met a man in a pub in New Ross, an auctioneer, and he had some thoughts on the matter:

'Do you know there's farmers around here with cars and combines, highly mechanized, modern milking parlours and all the rest of it, and thirty years ago I used to see 'em coming into New Ross in an ass cart.

It was the Common Market you see. Suddenly, back in the sixties and seventies, they found they were just making money, hand-over-fist. They couldn't help but make it. Men that'd been hard put to supply themselves with a donkey car a few years before were coming into this pub and ordering brandy — and not just any old brandy, it had to be the best — ordering it by the bottle and sitting and knocking it off.'

But it wasn't only down to the Common Market, although the farmers of Ireland did benefit greatly from it. It was Land Reform. It was the fact that, for the first time for eight hundred years — not since the first Norman invasion, in fact — the farmers owned their own land.

CHAPTER FIVE

We Take to the Rivers

T HE ESTATE OF WHICH my house was once a part was owned for many centuries by a number of different Protestant families. They extracted rents, for every piece of land and for every house; and the rents they extracted were just as much as they could possibly get. The landlords employed agents to collect the rents, and the more money the agents extracted the more they retained for themselves in commission. Rack renting, as it was called, was common all over Ireland. Tenants could be evicted at any time without notice, and were not compensated for improvements they had made. There were always others waiting only too eagerly to take their places when they were evicted. Therefore the agents were free to extract the highest rent that they could, leaving the farmer with just enough of his crop to live on in good years. When a bad year came along the farmers could not find the rent and so were kicked out, either to die on the roadside or emigrate to America or other countries. My nearest neighbour on my side of the river, Jimmy Walsh, who is an old man living alone in a tiny cabin, remembers being evicted from the family farm when he was a child. His father was lucky, and managed to find a cabin to rent near New Ross and a job in the maltings there, so he did not have to emigrate, and Jimmy is still here.

It was Jimmy to whom we turned when we wanted to buy a *prong*. The little clinker-built pram-dinghy, which we found belonged to the man we rented our house from, James Wharram, was reaching the end of its days. There are two sorts of traditional small open boats on our river (or our system of rivers, as the Barrow is one of three beautiful tidal rivers, the others being the Suir and the Nore): one is the *cot*, the other the *prong*. These are the upriver boats at least; there are other traditional types down in Waterford Harbour, nearer the sea.

The *cot* is a perilous little craft, serving the same purpose as the Welsh

37

coracle. A mere slip of a boat, with just enough buoyancy to support one man, she is worked in pairs: two *cots* with a man in each and a net between them. They are slowly paddled down or up the stream, and if a salmon swims into the net the men get it. The *prong* is a much more multi-purpose boat, and it was a *prong* we wanted. In section she looks like half a barrel; no keel or keelson, soft-wood planks spiked to grown curved elm or oak frames, with a transom stern and an upward-curving bow section making her look superficially like the West of Ireland *curach*. She is from fourteen to eighteen feet long, very stable, and has one great virtue: she can toboggan down the mud at low tide!

Jimmy Walsh, who is exactly the same age as I am (I am 76 as I write this) is a riverman. Having been evicted from the family farm as a child he was without a farm, so he worked for other people; but also he caught fish. Some *cot* and all *prong* men have licences to take salmon, and for most of his life Jimmy was such a man. He had owned a *prong* most of his life but he hasn't got one now.

So it was to Jimmy we went, asking for help and advice in buying a *prong*. They are rare now. Being planked with deal they do not last for ever. That they last as long as they do is because they are heavily pitched. Cylinders of hard pitch are liberated from road works, boiled down, and applied to the bottom.

The great *prong*-hunt began. It led us up many strange creeks and to many strange places. It led us to the cottage down the river from us, on our side, which stands by a little artificial harbour, with big lime kilns by it, and inhabited by an old couple who have lived there for all their lives. There was a *prong*, sleek and black and upside down on the grass looking like a stranded dolphin, but the old man would not sell her to us. 'One day my grandchildren might be needing her,' he said. The Harbour Board had just brought the electricity cable down to this place and established a fixed navigation light on the end of the quay. In return for permission to do this it had offered the couple to connect their house to the electricity. They would do this for nothing, and, being old-age pensioners, the couple would get their current free as well.

'When are they going to be doing it?' asked Jimmy.

'Not at all. We told 'em we're after gettin' along thus far without it and wouldn't change now,' said the man.

We fared further down the river, to Ballyhack, where there is a castle built by the Knights Templar but knocked about a bit by Oliver Cromwell.

There is also a beautiful little fishing harbour, where small half-decked fishing boats shelter from their work of drift-netting for salmon in the summer and herring in the winter, and there is Pat Carrol the boat builder. We went into that man's building shed, where he and his son and another man were working on building a massive, fifty-five-foot salmon boat. We admired her construction, and asked Mr Carrol about *prongs*. There were none available that he knew of, he said. There were *prongs* in the harbour but none for sale.

So we decided to try on the Kilkenny side. We went to see an old fishing pal of Jimmy's who lived in a kind of prefabricated one-roomed house on the hills overlooking the river. This house, or more correctly hut, had everything that a sensible bachelor would need for spiritual and physical refreshment. As we went in the door we were nearly knocked over by the heat, which was tropical. It emanated from a massive Aga stove at one end of the room. The rest of the space was taken up with an enormous double — nay treble, at least king-sized perhaps even emperor-sized — bed. There was just room in the corridor between this bed and the Aga and the walls to shuffle round it. Under the bed was a case of bottled soft drinks, to which we had frequent recourse, sitting on the bed and drinking out of the bottles. The mini-climate in there generated enormous thirst. Our host, a small, slight, fairly old man, sat in his shirt sleeves and gently perspired. Hung on the walls were a big picture of the Pope, another of the Sacred Heart, a Virgin and Child, and many cut-outs from girlie magazines that made even me blush to look at them. Our host had been a licensed salmon fisherman for many years, then, as licences became more expensive and harder to get, an unlicensed one, and now he was retired. Finding something strangely unsatisfying about the diet of soft drink, and positively wilting under the heat, we persuaded our man to come down to the local pub with us, and there we had a few drinks and enquired after *prongs*.

Armed with names and suggestions we left that place and scoured the countryside all along the Kilkenny side of the river. Everywhere we drew a blank. 'No — I'd never sell th'owd prong,' said one. 'The bailiffs are after taking mine,' said another. 'May God punish 'em!' And so on. So we gave it up and drove homewards feeling rather despondent.

'John boy, turn down to the left there,' said Jimmy, just before we got to the bridge that leads to New Ross. 'I haven't seen Jack Roche for a good many years. Like a word with him.'

Now Jack is a brother of Bob Roche of Duncannon, and Richie

Roche of New Ross (the man who took me to the bone setter). Jack owns a pub at Rosbercon, over the river from his brother Richie. Their father was a publican, a mighty man who left legends behind him when he died. We went into Jack's bar and had a drink, or two. Jack is a fine big friendly man and we got talking to him. Pub-crawling with Jimmy is a rewarding experience because, seemingly no matter how far from his home we roam, he is sure to meet old friends: generally ones whom he has not met for thirty years. But they recognize him, he recognizes them, and they are long-lost friends. We told Jack what we had been looking for.

'A *prong*?' he said. 'I've got one I'll sell you. Two hundred pounds.'

He led us over some marshes, down to the river, and there, lying in a little creek, lay a beautiful *prong*. We bought her there and then. Seek and ye shall find; but I suppose that if we added the cost of the beer that we had consumed during the search to the sum we paid she would not appear so much of a bargain.

The day we bought her was Saint Patrick's Day. We felt there must be something significant about that. The next day was pretty cold and windy, when Angela and I set out and walked to New Ross to collect our new boat. Jack Roche had promised to supply a pair of oars with her. We got to his pub, and took a dram or two to warm us up after the long cold walk, and another dram or two to fortify ourselves for the coming no doubt long cold row, and then Jack hauled the promised oars out from a shed at the back of his pub.

They were massive, enormous; they might have come out of a Roman galley. It took a strong man to lift one off the ground. They were much longer than the *prong* that they were meant to propel. As they were all there was, we laboriously lugged them down to the creek, got them aboard, slid the *prong* down the mud and jumped aboard.

By now, the wind, which was southerly and a dead header for us, had freshened to a half-gale. The tide was ebbing of course (we would never have tried to row home against the flood tide) and so we had wind-against-tide which always kicks up a choppy sea. Angela pulled the bow oar and I the stroke, as I found it was impossible to pull both oars myself because of their vast length. Angela had hardly ever pulled an oar in her life. 'Lift the blade out of the water,' I said, 'and lean right forward. Now drop the blade back in the water. No, hold it so the blade's upright. That's right. Now lean back — and *haul*!'

The conditions were not ideal for Lesson One in Rowing for Beginners.

But Angela struggled heroically, and the tide was with us if the wind was not. The up-curving bow of the little boat lifted well to the now quite considerable waves, and eventually we began to make some progress: painful, but progress.

'My hands are frozen,' said Angela.

'Never mind. Haul away — they'll soon warm up.' I did not tell her that my hands were frozen too. It was damned cold.

We managed to shoot New Ross bridge (the successor of the one built over that wide deep river to the orders of Earl William, Marshal of England, in 1210 AD) and we no doubt cut a strange figure as we wambled through New Ross — from time to time spinning round in a full circle, Angela occasionally being knocked flat on her back by the enormous oar. Suddenly I heard the sound of weeping behind me. I turned round and saw that Angela was not weeping because of the manifest misery of her position but out of sheer fury that she was not able to master that enormous oar. She doesn't like to be beat. Her hands were blue with cold.

'Look, there is a little harbour in the wall over there,' I said, pointing to the east bank where there was a tiny hole in the bank with several *cots* tied up in it. 'We're going in it.' We managed to get in, and got ashore.

'What are we going to do?'

'Go back to Jack's Bar, get a rum into you, and borrow a saw.'

So back we walked. We had whatever we had to warm us up; then we had whatever we had to prepare us for any privations to come. There were a couple of old river men in there and we talked *prongs* — and salmon, and nets, and bailiffs (those grim fellows who come zooming down our rivers in fast rubber speedboats to catch the unwary poacher).

I went out and strolled down to the river bank. The wind had died right down. The tide was still ebbing strongly but the river was beautifully calm. I went back to the pub. 'Come on,' I said to Angela. 'We'll go and tackle it again. There are another three hours of ebb — if we just sit still and do nothing it'll get us home.'

So Jack drove us back to the boat and we got aboard, not bothering to saw any bits off the oars as I wanted to take time over such a delicate process. Away we pulled again, warm and happy, and got back to our own little quay.

During the next few days we practised rowing the *prong*. They are tricky to row — having no keel they spin round very easily. We found that it was true what people said about them tobogganning down the mud. If we came

41

ashore at high tide and then wanted to launch at low tide, we just had to start the boat moving down the mud and get our bums aboard. She would then pick up speed and positively zoom down the steep soft mud, hit the water with a splash, and continue out into the river for many yards before stopping. We have since surprised many a guest by making them participate, unwarned, in this manœuvre .

The day came when we felt we were fit to come under the stares of the seamen and rivermen of New Ross again, and we decided to row into the town to go shopping. A strong tide bore us up to the outskirts of the town, and then we fairly bent to our oars. We made that *prong* move. We tied up to one of the town steps and went ashore, into Matty Ryan's Bar, to quench an honest thirst.

Two old rivermen were in there, quenching theirs. 'Did ye see that!' said one to the other. 'Did ye see that *prong*? There was a man and a young-one in it — and I've never seen a *prong* moving so fast! Like hell they were going!' Angela and I sat and modestly sipped our beers. We didn't own up it was us.

We did without our car for nearly a year once. We left it in Wales for the use of one of my kids, and did all our shopping, and pubbing, in the *prong*. She is certainly the most useful article we have ever owned, and we have had endless use and pleasure out of her. We used to make a habit, and will again, of going drift-wooding in the *prong* every Saturday, up or down the river. We gathered together great rafts of wood, lashed it all together with rope, shoved it in the water and towed it home to our quay. We hauled it out and stacked it inside the lime kilns to dry for a few weeks. Then one day we would ask John-Joe for the loan of his tractor and trailer and carry it up to the house.

My daughter Kate and her husband Julian came to see us once and we decided to go camping in the *prong*. We loaded up a tent and other gear and slipped off from the end of the quay an hour or two after high water. The tide, and a little gentle work from the oars, took us downstream and, as we had started late in the afternoon, we arrived at the village and little fishing harbour of Cheek Point at the confluence of the Barrow and the Suir, before low tide. As we intended to go up the Suir we could proceed no further: the ebb in the Suir would be against us and the tides in our rivers are strong enough to preclude rowing against them unless you have a very good reason to do so.

Cheek Point, like all the little fishing villages of Waterford Harbour, is extremely picturesque: the artificial harbour is full of small fishing boats, the village is pretty. There is a green sward between the harbour and the houses, with a big sign in the middle of it which says 'No Camping'. We went into the pub and asked the landlord if he could suggest anywhere for us to pitch a tent for the night. 'Yes,' he said. 'Shove it out there on the green.'

'Where?' I asked.

'Over there, look, beside the No Camping sign.'

Deciding that a second opinion might be desirable, I went out and strolled over to where a couple of old men sat on a bench. One of them had a patch over one eye and looked like a very respectable retired pirate.

'Do you think it would be all right if I pitched a tent here for the night?' I asked.

'Pitch it where you like,' they both said.

'But it says there, no camping.'

'Take no notice.'

So there we camped.

I wanted to find out something in Cheek Point. Years ago I used to sail as Third Hand on a sailing barge, the *Cambria*, owned by Everards, its captain, Master Bob Roberts, now alas no longer with us. Bob once told me the story about how, when he was a young sailor aboard a brigantine, and the brigantine had gone on the rocks, he and a young friend had put their money together and bought an ancient and very leaky schooner in Liverpool. They knew that if they could get the boat round to the east coast of England they could get her repaired, by a friend who owned a shipyard. But, being short of cash, they decided to earn some with her first.

They bought a load of coal, on tick, and sailed across the Irish Sea to Ireland. They knew they could always make a modest profit by doing that. They beached the schooner somewhere on the south coast, unloaded the coal into horse carts at low tide and sold it. This gave them a modest profit; but they had lost a sail on the voyage, and found other defects that desperately needed fixing, so they sailed back to England or Wales, bought another load of coal and sailed it to Ireland. This went on for many months and they took a score or so of freights of coal, but they were on a hiding to nowhere. 'The Irish Sea's like this, John,' said Bob. 'There's always a gale blowing, either up it or down it.' All the money they earned they had to spend on gear, and the old schooner began to leak more and more. Finally, on the way home from dropping another load of coal at Arklow, they met a ferocious gale, and for two days and nights the two boys (they were only eighteen) got no sleep, nor time to eat, as one always had to steer and the other to pump. They were driven round to Waterford Harbour in a sinking condition. A pilot came out and led them into Cheek Point, where we were now camping, and told them to beach the ship on the mud. I asked the old man with the patch over one eye if he knew anything about the boat. For answer he led me along the shore, and there, lying in the mud, were the bones of a small schooner.

Well, we camped there that night, our tent actually made fast to the No Camping sign, and next morning started rowing up the River Suir, a large tidal river, though not as wide or magnificent as our Barrow (how could it be?). We soon got to Waterford where we went ashore to explore the city.

Waterford was already a city when the first Norman invasion occurred, having been built by the Vikings, and retains a fine, rather medieval atmosphere. Up until a few decades ago, when a dock strike that went on for ten years nearly killed it, the port of Waterford was important. The strike nearly knocked it out, except for the container trade operated by the Bell shipping line (containers don't need dockers).

Returning to our boat, we continued to row upstream. The time came when we had to start thinking about finding a camping site again; the *prong* was too small for us all to sleep aboard. But we had reached a part of the river where there seemed to be nothing but huge reed beds on both sides. There was no way through the reed beds, and they were flooded by the high tide.

I began to think that we would have to drop downriver again to find dry ground. Then I suddenly noticed a tiny break in the reeds on the south bank. We rowed over to it and discovered a narrow channel through the reeds just wide enough to accommodate the boat. We wound our way up it, having to push ourselves along with the oars because there was not room to deploy them properly, and suddenly — after a long and winding passage — the creek opened out into a tiny harbour, about as big as a small house, in which lay seven *cots*.

'Look, the Seven Dwarfs live here!' said Angela. And indeed it looked like it: there these seven little boats lay, end-on to the bank, and next to each one was a rack of poles with salmon nets hung on them to dry. The creek ended here, and we were still surrounded by tall reeds. But there was one piece of reedless ground above the water just big enough to erect the tent on. 'We'll have to be away by six tomorrow morning,' I said, 'because this tump will be flooded.' So next day we scrambled, and took the ebb back down to Waterford, attended Mass in the Augustinian church, dropped down to the Barrow and anchored for three hours under a great cliff over which peregrine falcons soared. Some of us had a swim (but not me), and then we let the flood take us up the Barrow to our home again.

What beautiful rivers these are! How completely unspoiled. In any other country in Europe rivers like the three we live on, the Nore, the Suir and the Barrow (the 'Three Sisters' they are called), would be crowded with pleasure boats. We hardly ever see one. If we go upstream (and we have, often) we can either turn left, beyond New Ross, up the Nore, and get as far as the limit of navigation at Inistioge; or we can go straight on up the Barrow to a place named Saint Mullins. Either journey is breath-takingly beautiful. The rivers, narrower up here, wind between the great gorges they have cut through the hills, the banks of which are wooded with fine trees, lost, lonely and uninhabited. I have seen most of the great rivers of the world — the Bhramaputra, the Orange, the Mississippi and the Tigris — but nothing as beautiful, or as wild and unspoiled, as the Three Sisters, on the banks of one of which I have the happiness to live. Lucky is the man or woman who lives in Ireland, if they can make a living that is. It is the most beautiful country in the world.

CHAPTER SIX

✥

The Singing Pubs

OF COURSE, AFTER I HAD COME TO LIVE in Ireland I had to go and look up the old friends that I had made before, in the pony and cart days. I had no expectations that they would remember me: after all, it was fourteen years since I had seen them and then it was only a fleeting encounter. So Angela and I drove back to Duncannon, and up to the great fort. The gates were open and we drove in. A few soldiers were sauntering about, and, just over the moat, we found two men deep in conversation. One was dressed as a colonel, the other was a civilian with a snow-white beard. I drew up beside them. 'Does Paddy Burke live here still?' I asked them.

'John!' roared the man with the beard, who looked something like an ancient sea captain in the sailing ship days. 'You ould divil — where've you sprung from?'

I realized then that Paddy's beard, vivid red when I had known him, had turned white over the years. Otherwise he looked just the same. Paddy introduced us to the colonel, who was commanding some unit resting down at Duncannon after a spell on the Ulster border, and then took us into his house to meet Phyllis his wife. She remembered me too, immediately. You can very seldom get out of an Irish house without eating and drinking something. That we did, and there was a warm and friendly welcome in the Burke kitchen.

The fort where we had been reunited is of enormous historical interest. Built on a rocky promontory that juts out into Waterford Harbour, its guns could completely cover the deep channel up which ships sailed to New Ross or Waterford. It withstood several sieges, failed to withstand a few, and was active as a fortification right up to the Second World War (what the Irish called 'The Emergency' because they could not bring themselves to call it a war), when anti-aircraft guns and searchlights were installed in it, and coastal defence guns too. Now, alas, the army has given it up, and I no longer have the fun of being a guest in the barracks bar and imagining myself (nice and briefly) in the army again. The place is up for sale but nobody seems to want it.

Well, we ate and drank, and Paddy suggested we go to the pub, to meet various of his sons and sons-in-law who were in from the fishing. We strolled out through the great gates, past the half-buried cannons, and came to the very hotel into which I had booked myself and Dolly the horse fourteen years before. The hotel had long since burned down, and been bought by one Bob Roche, who had turned the stable and coach houses wherein Dolly and my cart had been stabled into a bar. We came to a massive door with bronze hinges, opened it and were met by the sound of music. In front of us on our left was a long bar with a very pretty young woman behind it, and hung up on the wall behind her, or resting on a range of shelves, a jumble of objects of nautical interest: objects which had obviously been brought home from the seven seas by home-coming sailors. It was very much a sailors' pub. Hard round to our left the bar made a right-angle turn, leaving just a little space between it and the front wall. In this space sat the people making the music. One of them was an extremely pretty young woman with a mane of jet-black hair coming down below her waist. She was playing a tin whistle with great dexterity, with her small, very shapely fingers. Next to her sat a tall, spare, distinguished-looking old man with what seemed to me to be a noble face surmounted by grey hair. He wore no hat. He was playing a violin with great verve and at high speed, as indeed he had to, to keep up with the girl on the whistle, who must have been some fifty years his junior. Then there was a plumpish fresh-faced young man playing that instrument known as the *uilaenn* pipes, small bagpipes, the air of which is provided by bellows strapped to the inside of the upper arm of the player. They are widespread in Ireland but I have only seen them elsewhere in Northumberland, where they are called 'the small pipes'. Then there was a youngish, tall, black-haired man with a thin, strikingly handsome face playing the *bodhrán*, the small drum. The sound they were all making was spirited in the extreme.

I asked Paddy Burke who they all were. 'Well the young-one with the whistle is Liz Cassidy, only we all call her Liz King. That's her maiden name and she and her sister Mary were famous as children for the music and dancing. She's won the all-Ireland championship on the whistle several times. The fiddler is Jim Smith. He's retired now but he was huntsman with the fox-hounds all his life. The piper is Paddy Molloy; he's a sailor in the Bell

47

Line ships. The man with the *bodhrán* is Bob Roche himself, the landlord here. That's his wife behind the bar.'

In the narrow body of the barroom maybe a dozen men sat on stools or sat around the warm coal fire. Nearly all of them were fishermen or seamen and most of them seemed to be either Paddy's sons or his sons-in-law. His two sons I had met before, when they were little boys pulling their socks on in Paddy's kitchen ready to go to school. Anthony was a strapping young man with a big red beard, such as his father had had when I first met him. He was mate of a big beam trawler fishing out of Kilmore Quay. His brother, Hugh, still only a teenager, was tall, with a handsome face and a mop of curly dark hair. He worked at that time aboard one of the small half-deckers that fish from Duncannon, for salmon in the summer and herring in the autumn and winter.

True Irish country music (not the commercialized stuff you often hear in Dublin) strikes some strong chord in me and I believe it does the same thing to Angela. I have observed in other people that it either has this effect on you or it leaves you cold. It was a long time before we could tear ourselves away from Bob's Bar, and before we did so we found that the musicians played there every Saturday evening and they still do. We took to drifting in there on a Saturday night and soon became firm friends with them all. One day Jim Smith said to me, 'John, you and Angela seem to like the music. Why don't you come over my part of the country? Come to Carrig-on-Bannow one Wednesday evening. There's a good *craic* to be had there.' *Craic* has been anglicized into 'crack' and means 'fun'.

Accordingly, one day we did. We made our way south until we hit a road called the Duncannon Line, built by the British army after the 1798 rebellion so that soldiers from the fort at Duncannon would be able to get to Wexford town more quickly than they had done during the rebellion when they had failed to save the lives of very many Protestants. Taking the shortest route, the road is therefore dead straight for most of its length, and if it were not for the fact that the Romans never got here one would immediately take it for a Roman road.

We drove east along it until we came to Wellington Bridge. This is a busy village near the bridge over the River Corock which runs, right at that very point, into Bannow Bay, a widening tidal estuary most rich in wading birds, some of it being a bird reserve. On the west bank of the estuary, and you can see it from the bridge, is a collection of ruined medieval buildings called Clonmines. In a small area there are three castles: one the former stronghold of the Suttons, one of the Purcells and one of the Fitz Henrys; and also the ruins of three churches. One of these was part of an Augustinian Abbey and another of a Dominican Friary (both were suppressed and destroyed during Henry VIII's time); and further down the river on that bank is a huge ruined Cistercian abbey, called Tintern after the sister house in Gloucestershire. Over the estuary from Clonmines is an abandoned silver mine dating from Tudor times. When I first saw it, Tintern Abbey was completely deserted, desolate and uncared for. Now it is being done up by the equivalent of the Board of Works. If it were in any other country in Europe it would be flooded with tourists.

Turning right off the Duncannon Line we followed a small road along the bank of the estuary, and then turned right again to come to a bleak and deserted headland with nothing on it but a ruined church and a graveyard. This is all that is left of the important town of Bannow, which sent two members to parliament long after it had completely disappeared, having been overwhelmed by sands and the sea.

After taking in this desolation we turned and drove east for a mile or two until we came to our destination: the village of Carrig-on-Bannow. We had been summoned to Colfer's Bar, and for a while we had to search for it. There was a fine big Catholic church, one street with a score or so of small houses, and three shops. True, the latter could also double as pubs, as often happens in small Irish villages. We went into one shop, which did indeed have a bar at the back of it, and enquired for Colfer's Bar. 'There, over the road,' said the man. Over the road was a small building which did, indeed, have a tiny shop-front to it. We went in and found ourselves in a very small room with a counter on one side and shelves behind this stocked with groceries. It reminded me of a village shop from about the 1950s. A screen cut this room off from another room, and the counter was extended beyond this screen. We went through a door in the screen and found ourselves in a slightly larger room with a concrete floor and a bar — the extension of the counter of the shop — round two sides of it. There were some wooden benches along two walls and some bar stools up against the bar, and a few rough chairs. Jim Smith sat in one of them, his violin case on the floor beside him, and Cathy, his wife, sat beside him. There were two or three other people there. It was very quiet.

'Glad you were able to make it,' said Jim. And Cathy told us a funny story of which she has a bottomless store; I have heard hundreds since and never the same one twice.

The door opened and a very large man walked in, a fine-looking, quite old man of Falstaffian figure — white hair, a big white moustache, patriarchal. With him was a beautiful motherly lady with her hair piled up on top of her head and wearing somewhat flamboyant clothes. They sat down beside us. 'This is Andy Monahan,' Jim told us, 'and his wife Bridie. They live just down the road from here.' He tried to explain to them who we were.

Another very tall and large man entered and joined us. He, it appeared, was Jack McCutcheon. 'He keeps order here; he's our MC,' said Andy, introducing us. 'As if anybody could keep order in this place,' murmured Jack.

People were beginning to trickle in now. Young people, old people, families with children. Whatever the law may be in Ireland there does not seem to be any inhibition about children in pubs, and better-behaved children you will never find. It is a pleasure to see them there. There was a buzz of conversation. Everybody knew everybody else. And there was a sort of expectancy in the air.

'Well then Andy,' said Jim, 'shall we give it a go?'

He took his violin out of its case and began to tune it. Then he put it under his chin and began to play, a serious look upon his thin, good-looking and rather noble face. He hadn't bothered to take his cigarette out of his mouth.

Andy was fossicking about in his capacious pockets. He pulled out a mouth organ, then another, then a couple more, and put them on the table. He selected one and began to play. It was some lively jig, slip-jig, reel or hornpipe: my musical ignorance is such that I have never learned to tell the difference, but, like all the traditional music one hears in Ireland it was most definitely Irish. You hear similar melodies in the Highlands of Scotland and in Northumberland, but the feeling they have to them is quite different. Bridie produced two spoons and rattled out a rhythm with them with great skill.

A young man got up and went outside, and came in again carrying a *bodhrán* in a canvas cover. He took it out and began to play. A girl pulled a tin whistle out of her handbag and joined in too. Perhaps half a dozen reels, jigs, hornpipes or whatever were played and then the musicians broke off for a drink.

It was then that Jack McCutcheon came into his own. In a formal and very authoritative way he called upon a pretty young girl to sing. She sang

'The Fields of Athenry', which Angela finds rather hackneyed and sentimental but I, sentimental old fool that I am, find moving, particularly when sung by a lovely young girl. Then, one after another, we were all called upon to contribute, in one way or another, to the evening's jubilation.

I watched McCutcheon with the greatest respect, for the job he was doing required tact yet authority, and a great knowledge of protocol. Under his stern command none of us could escape singing, or playing an instrument, or reciting a poem, or getting up and doing a dance, and yet nobody's nose got put out of joint.

'Come on Johnnie,' said Jack to a dapper man who leant up against the bar with a smart check suit on and a trilby hat with jay's wing feathers on the side of it. 'Sing us the Bunnie Song, Johnnie.'

And Johnnie, after suitable cajoling, sang a song of his own composition, a parody of 'My Bonnie lies over the Ocean', which was far wittier and funnier then the original. Then, after even more cajoling, he was persuaded to dance a hornpipe, which he did to extremely fast music provided by Jim and Andy. Arms held tight to sides, gaze straight ahead, hat on head, he danced extremely skilfully and intricately for a few minutes and then stopped. We all realized that that was it; he had given his contribution for that evening.

I have heard the greatest professional musicians in the world playing sublime music in great concert halls and it is a splendid thing, but it is entirely passive. You are not allowed to be passive at Colfer's Bar. Indeed, it takes iron self-control to stop oneself from getting up and dancing wildly. Sometimes my own self-control breaks down. Sometimes even that small measure of self-control needed to prevent me from leaping up and dancing on the nearest table breaks down too! Sometimes the table breaks down! I am a sore embarrassment to my friends. But much is excused by age.

Now, Angela has a lovely voice, and a voice divinely-made for the singing of folk song. Jim Smith had already discovered this and she had to sing 'Oh My Name is Mol Malone' and 'Where Only the Rivers Run Free'. Jim Smith, although he spent his life hunting the fox and breaking horses, is a connoisseur of folk song. He is a purist, and his face shows his displeasure when people sing modern rubbish — if it goes on too long, he will get up, put his violin in its case, and walk out. As there are three bars in Carrick — and he is more than welcome in all of them — this is not the ultimate sacrifice.

But that night there was nothing to bring a frown to Jim's brow. After an hour or two of warming up with the music, and being mellowed by the stout and the rum which he prefers, Jim was persuaded to sing one of the hundred-odd ballads he knows. These are mostly about dreadful shipwrecks of long ago, when sailing ships, in from the Atlantic, used to mistake the Hook Lighthouse for the Eddystone, round up beyond it, thinking they were heading for Plymouth Harbour, and sail straight on to the rocks of the Bannow shore. These ballads were composed by people ashore who wished to pay tribute both to the lifeboat crews who risked their lives to save strangers, and often lost them in the attempt, and to the gallantry and sacrifice of the sailors themselves. The ballads tend to be rather long, and sometimes contain long lists of names of long-dead mariners. Also, as the subject is lugubrious, the tunes tend to be pretty sombre and I am sometimes amazed that the younger and more impatient members of our company, long conditioned by modern pop songs, are so patient. But they know the rules. You do not interrupt, whisper witticisms to your companion, yawn, cough, belch, or make any other untoward noises, when Jim Smith is singing. You listen in appropriate silence and at the end render fitting applause. I find all this easy to do, not only because I love these ancient ballads, but because Jim has a fine and splendid voice, and, having sailed in commercial sailing ships myself from time to time, I have an appreciation of the subjects of the songs.

Bridie Monahan, who has got to be my favourite grandmother, plays the spoons and can rattle a rhythm out of an empty Guinness bottle. Her true talent, though, is as a poet and when asked to recite, all she has to do is close her eyes and wait for her muse to aid her. Andy, her famous husband, he of the great white moustache (in those days at least — some whim has caused him to shave it down to a mere streak across his upper lip in recent years) puts his mouth organ to his lips and plays as even Larry Adler would be proud to play. He plays that simple instrument with skill, speed, passion and love. His pockets are full of mouth organs and, whenever the other musicians strike up an air, he fumbles in them for the one in the correct key and without a pause joins in.

As Angela and I drove home that night, or rather next morning, we expressed to each other our amazement at a country where you can get together a roomful of ordinary working country people — farm workers, retired farm workers, lorry drivers, road workers, the unemployed — who can show as much talent as we had just heard and seen.

Angela, who is Irish of course, said it was because we were in Ireland.

The Irish were like that: a race of bards and poets, singers and dancers and musicians. I am not so sure. I was privileged to encounter the last sparks of the true Merry England in some of the pubs around my old home in Suffolk, and I have a feeling that England too, before the reign of the Puritans, could have provided just this sort of conviviality. But, it may be argued, Ireland was conquered by the Puritans too — in fact even more thoroughly than England was. In 1654 Colonel Sadleir, governor of Wexford after the Cromwellian capture of the city, humbly requested that the Commissioners of the Commonwealth of England for the Affairs of Ireland should send 'positive orders . . . to ye Justices and Commissioners there that they grant no Lycences nor permit any of the Irish nation, upon any pretense whatsoever, to keep an Inne or Alehouse.' And his request was granted.

England had its Restoration; after the return of Charles II some merriment was allowed, and no doubt music and singing and dancing came back into the countryside again. But then came the Industrial Revolution, and the heart was sucked out of the English countryside. The few people who were left there lived in the direst poverty (except the squires of course), and the spirit left it, to be kept alive only in one or two little pockets of resistance such as a remote parish here and there in the Suffolk coastal area, or the South Downs country of Sussex, in the Yorkshire Dales, or in Northumberland.

What is amazing about County Wexford, and in fact any part of the Irish countryside east of the River Shannon, is that the spirit of the people was not completely crushed. Indeed, it arose triumphant! The history of Ireland is one long list of crushing defeats of the Irish people by various British armies. But the Cromwellian invasion was of quite a different order. After the storming of Drogheda, Cromwell wrote: 'The officers were knocked on the head, every tenth man of the soldiers killed and the rest shipped to the Barbadoes . . . I think we put to the sword altogether about 2,000 men.' He forgot to mention the hundreds of women and children who were similarly accommodated. But he added that this was all done by the Spirit of God and 'therefore it is right that God should have all the glory.' Let us hope that the Almighty was pleased with this little acknowledgement.

In Wexford town the story was repeated. The tract *A very full and Particular Relation*, written by a participant, tells us all about it. Like all the members of the parliamentary army he seems to have suffered from a positive loathing of the Irish people and, more particularly, the ancient faith to which, amazingly, they still adhered. After the castle, which was

53

the strong point of the defence, had been handed over by the Royalist (and Irish) defenders through the treachery of the governor, he describes what happened next:

> 'Seeing that the righteous hand of God was upon such a Towne and People, we thought not good nor just to restraine off our souldiers for their right of Pillage, nor from doing execution upon the Enemy, where the entrance was by force, and a resistance endeavoured although too late. There was more sparing of lives (of the Souldiery part of the Enemy here) than at Drogheda, yet of their Souldiery and Townsmen here were about 1,500 slaine (or drowned in boats sunk by the multitude and weight of people pressing into them). It was a place settled the most deep in superstition and darknesse that I have seene or heard of, and a people zealous against anything of better light.'

Nor were the unarmed priests spared. All the Augustinian friars were slaughtered, and their Friary desecrated:

> 'God visited both the deceivers and the deceived together. Of their Priests (which deceived and led them) were many slaine. Some (I heard of) came forth holding Crucifixes before them, and conjouring our Souldiers (for his sake that saved us all) to save their lives; yet our Souldiers would not owne their dead images for our living Saviour, but struck them dead with their Idols. Many of their Priests being got together in a Church of the Towne . . . were slaine together by our Souldiers about their Altar.'

The chronicler says nothing of the 200 women and children who were slaughtered in the market place in one well-recorded incident. But another Cromwellian letter writer, Mr Hugh Peters, writing to a friend in London, describes how 'the hand of God wonderfully appears,' for in their flight over the water '2,000 were killed and drowned.'

Of course Ireland was a godsend to Oliver Cromwell. He could in no way find the money for his soldiers' back pay, and so he simply took all land belonging to Catholics in Ireland east of the Shannon and paid them with that. Catholic landowners were simply told to get themselves over the Shannon. 'To Hell or Connaught' was the command given to them. Many were shipped off to slavery in America. In the town records we hear of a Captain John Norris obtaining 'leave to transport men, women and young women (not under 18), vagrants, idlers and beggars to the plantations in America. Those transported by him out of Wexford, Ross and Kilkenny 100 in number. 25 October.'

The landless Irish were allowed to remain, provided they worked for Protestants. Some converted to Protestantism, and we read of a petition from 'the Irish inhabitants of Wexford, setting forth their Resolution to heare the word of God read and preacht unto them.' Maybe they thought that conversion was a better fate than transportation.

So I find it rather hard to see where my friends at Bob Roche's Bar, or Colfer's, or many another, came from. All the land of County Wexford that was not already owned by English Protestants was taken up by Cromwell's soldiers. Anyone not working for these was either forced across the Shannon, into the barren rocks of Connaught, or shipped off to American plantations. How did the Catholic ancestors of Bridie and Andy Monahan, Jack McCutcheon, Johnnie Bennet and all the rest of them survive? And how on earth did their descendants retain their sense of fun and humour, their faith, their oral and musical culture, as they have done? For Cromwell was not only not the first Englishman to come to Ireland to slay, repress and to conquer, he was also not the last.

CHAPTER SEVEN

~

Our Neighbourhood

BUT WHERE AM I? — I must get back to our own house. I do not wish to give the impression that Angela and I spent, or spend, all our time pub-crawling. In fact I don't believe we go to a pub more than once a month on average. Angela does brew the most magnificent beer, though; and this may well be the reason why people tend to ramble down our rough track.

Two tracks lead to our house: one, called 'the New Road', which was made in the 1920s when the estate was carved up among the tenants, is motorable, and the other isn't. If you walk back along the motorable one you eventually pass the garden hedge of Killowen House, a large and beautiful Georgian mansion the former owners of which once owned the countryside for miles around. Michael and Anne Ryan live in it now with their three fine and clever children who pass all their exams and go to university. Michael is a newscaster on RTE television and has to drive to Waterford every day, where his office is; Anne runs a public relations business.

Just beyond this mansion, over the lane on the right, is the Whitty house. Here Johnnie and Mary Whitty have brought up a family of eleven fine healthy children. Johnnie is the hardest-working man I think I have ever met.

With such a large family he considers he must build up a good business to leave to them all, and not only does he farm his own farm intensively and milk a big herd of cows, he also 'sets' land (the local way of saying he rents it to other people) and has a large fleet of machinery which he and his sons use to do contract work for other people. The whole family are indefatigable. The boys, from an early age, are always to be seen either in the cab of a tractor, or else underneath one, or some other piece of machinery, for they are all good mechanics. If any new machine is invented the Whitties buy one as soon as it hits the market. As the children grow up they tend to leave home; the oldest boy went to Australia, and within an hour of getting off the plane had got himself a very good, well-paid job as a mechanic.

My neighbours are good farmers. They are mixed farmers, in the old, traditional style, and yet they are not out of date or old-fashioned. New inventions, such as the big round hay-bale, and big-bale silage, were adopted around here long before they were widespread in England. But the farmers here have not gone in for monoculture like English arable farmers have.

They all have livestock, most of them a flock of sheep which they feed, in the winter, on turnips or other root crops (an excellent practice, for the improvement of the land); most of them milk a herd of cows (all of them have some cattle); and most of them grow a variety of crops. They grow fine wheat.

If we wander up the other lane that comes to our house, happily not motorable, we go by a wood, up a hill, along a green lane with high hedges on either side of it, until we come out into the open, and get grand views both up and down the great winding River Barrow in the distance beneath us.

We pass by a deserted cottage, very lonely and remote. A young man lived in it when we first came here; both his mother and father had died and he lived all alone. Some years ago he went to England and, like thousands of his countrymen, has never come back. Then, on the left, is an old deserted farmhouse, with smashed windows swinging in the wind. This belonged until recently to our other good neighbour, John-Joe Hunt. It has now been bought by a Waterford man who intends one day to do it up and live in it. Then there is a little grove of trees and beyond them the tiny cottage, or cabin, of Jimmy Walsh, the man who helped us buy the *prong*. Although Jimmy lives quite alone he is seldom lonely because the world is full of his friends. People go down and sit by his little wood fire and talk with him; or he goes up to Long's Bar, our nearest pub, and has a pint or two; or he gets a lift into New Ross and meets friends there. If any of the local farmers wants another pair of hands to help, Jimmy is always there — and it is a good man who can keep up with him in the way of farm work or any hard manual labour. Jimmy shipped aboard a sailing ship when he was a young boy and made many voyages to South Wales, loading coal. Then for most of his life he managed a farm for a widow-lady. Now he is supposed to be retired.

Next we come to the hamlet of Dunganstown, where there are more ruins than houses. There must have been a considerable community here a couple of hundred years ago. There are now three good big modern farm-houses. One of the farms is famous, certainly at least in the United States. For here it was that the great-grandfather of John F. Kennedy, President of the United States, was born and brought up. Now the occupants inhabit a large farmhouse, built perhaps about 1900, but between it and the road is the older typical Irish cabin: just a small single-storeyed cottage, or hut really. The walls are made of stone held together with mud-mortar; the roof was once of thatch but is now of corrugated iron. So the Kennedy family went from this to the White House. Pat Kennedy lives down a lane, something like ours, right on the river, and farms there. In the old Kennedy house lives Mary Anne Ryan, who looks after two children, the sons of her late sister; both parents of the boys unfortunately died. She 'sets' the land — that is, lets it out — to other farmers, but she does keep some pedigree Hereford cattle because that is the tradition in the family, and one of the boys has a small flock of sheep. She keeps the land — and the 'Kennedy Homestead', with its presidential associations — in trust for the two small boys. I asked her once if she had ever thought of exploiting the site by attracting tourists to it and trying to make a little money from it, but she said she felt it was up to the boys to decide to do that or not when they became of age. As it is, there is a little sign saying 'Kennedy Homestead' stuck to the end of the historic building, half-hidden in ivy, and during the summer a small trickle of American tourists find their way to it. But there is practically nothing to see when they get there: a tiny room with a tin roof and a few pictures on the walls. No authority will pay for the tin roof to be replaced by the original thatch even. Yet the fact is that the lanes are so small and narrow around here that a flush of tourists to the place would be a great embarrassment. Anyway, there is Kennedy Park just a couple of miles away. Here a large estate has been purchased and planted up as one of the finest arboreta in the world. There is hardly a tree that can be made to grow in temperate climates that is not growing here. It is an astonishing place, but it is grossly under-used. Tree-lovers and people trying to learn about trees should come here from all parts of the world; but you can visit it and walk all round it on a fine day and perhaps see nobody at all, at the most half a dozen.

If you keep walking east from Dunganstown, within a mile you pass a couple of bungalows — it is all very sparsely populated — and then arrive at our thriving centre of Ballykelly. Here there is a Catholic church, big but only just big enough to contain us all (if you don't get there fairly early, sometimes you cannot get in), the presbytery in which lives Father Robert Mitchell, who has the cure of our souls, and, along the road, Seamus Long's Bar. We had driven past this building a dozen times when we first got here before we realized it was a bar at all. The Longs, like many good publicans, run a small farm as well as the pub, and therefore can talk to their customers about the things that interest them. Most of the habitués spend their evenings there playing cards. There is very much a family atmosphere and a stranger entering is an object of wonder. Jimmy Walsh has his own particular bar stool at one end of the bar and it is a gross dereliction of custom and good manners for anybody else to sit on it when Jimmy wants it, although he is much too polite to point this out.

If you walk south from here you come to the hamlet — or village perhaps — of Whitechurch where there is a Protestant church. On the second Sunday of every month a parson comes out from New Ross to take a service there. There is a scattering of Protestants in our parish, and the Protestant church may have only half a dozen or a dozen in the congregation whereas Ballykelly will have several hundred. The Protestants cover all social groups and classes but the majority are Anglo-Irish. Their ancestors probably came over with Cromwell's forces and were given grants of land. Some though, it is said, are the descendants of *soupers*. In times of famine starving people were offered soup — but only if they were willing to become Protestants. Some of them did, most of them didn't. The Anglo-Irish tend to live in the big old mansions that are common in the countryside, but the land of these old estates has been taken from them under the various Land Reform Acts that were passed from 1870 onwards. The estates were left with just the land that the owners were actually farming under their own hand; all tenanted land was purchased from them by the government and sold on to the tenants. Many of these 'West Brits', as they are sometimes called, have horses and therefore one hears of the 'horse-Protestants'. One also hears of 'left-footers', for it is alleged that Protestants dig by pushing the spade into the ground with their left foot, while Catholics use their right. I don't know how much serious research has gone into discovering if this theory is supported by fact.

But this I must say: in ten years of living in this country, and of travelling nearly all over it, I have never encountered the slightest prejudice or bad feeling between Catholics and Protestants. When the roof blew off a Protestant church near here it was the Catholics who raised most of the money to put it on again. It just doesn't matter what religion you are here, or if you have no religion at all: nobody gives a damn. Nobody ever even *asks* you: that would be the height of bad manners. But it is surprising how soon everybody finds out.

Harold Warren lives in a large old farmhouse, surrounded by many big barns and other large buildings. A tall screen of Scots pines shelters the group of buildings from the east. Harold's daughter, Patricia, lives in a converted mill building with her husband Roger and their baby, and the pair of them have substantially taken over the farm now Harold is semi-retired. They concentrate on sheep and have a very large flock of them. I went to see Harold the other day to ask him about old times. I met him in the yard and we had to shout to each other over the noise of several hundred ewes which were busy lambing in some of the big buildings around us.

He led me into the farmhouse, which was furnished with good quality but massive Victorian furniture, and I started to ask him questions.

'No, listen,' he said. 'What will you take? I have whiskey or stout.'

Whiskey it was, but Mr Warren contented himself with fizzy lemonade. I asked him about Whitechurch, which had got its name apparently because there was a cell of the white-robed Cistercian monks of Dunbrody Abbey here.

'Whitechurch was a small town when I was a boy,' he told me.

Now the place has perhaps a dozen houses in it, the little half-used church: no pub, no shop. It did have a shop but it closed down a year ago because the owner found the VAT nonsense too much to bear. Now if you are an old age pensioner without a car you must either get a lift into town to buy a postage stamp or go without.

But Harold told me that it was once quite otherwise. 'There were two shops,' he said, 'a blacksmith — and he employed a man — two carpenter's shops — and they both employed people — a dispensary, a dress-maker and a tailor, and later on a garage. There was once also a pub. There was a barracks [he meant a police station] but it was burnt down in the Troubles. Whitechurch was a thriving place.'

Part of the reason why it was thriving was the Warren family itself. Harold's father was a man of enormous resource. In the First World War (which Harold is old enough to remember well) the Warren farm employed thirty men and probably as many women. The men got nine shillings a week, the women far less. 'Two women did nothing else but cook for them all — they had their own dining room over there.'

The farm then, as now, was 127 acres in extent: certainly not a large enough acreage to employ sixty people. But Harold's father had established numerous small enterprises: they cured bacon and hams, killing twenty-five heavy hogs every week; they killed their own sheep and used the tallow to make candles; during the First World War they made 'tea' out of carrots for heaven's sake, on a very big scale; and they also grew tobacco and cured it. These commodities could not then be obtained from abroad. They had a properly equipped sawmill for which they would buy and fell trees from all around the district, a carpenter's shop, coach-builder's shop, blacksmith, paint shop; and they made and produced farm carts, light carriages, farm gates, hurdles and much else. They also had a travelling threshing set pulled by steam engine, and threshed the corn for other farmers in the district.

When Harold and his brother Sam took over from their father, Sam ran the industrial enterprises and Harold the farm. On the farm were six heavy horses, a dozen cows just to give milk and butter for all the workers, a flock of sheep and fifty sows. Very often there would be five hundred fattening pigs. Up until 1919 all the food for the stock had to be produced from the farm; after that date the co-op opened in Campile (four miles away) and some supplements could be bought from there. The land of the farm must have been enormously fertile, from the dung of all those animals.

They ran, at first, a horse van to deliver all the produce: bacon and ham, candles, tobacco, carrot tea and all the rest of it. Later came a motor van, with a bigger radius.

'You must have made a lot of money with all this?' I said.

'No, we never did. But we made a living — we survived.'

And, he might have added, they gave a living to many more people; they helped to keep that countryside alive.

The reason for the candles, of course, was not only because they had tons of fat to dispose of from the sheep and pigs that they killed, but because there was no electric light in the countryside. In the two wars you could not even get paraffin.

'Rural electricity came in 1937,' he said. 'But we had electricity before then.' In the early 1930s they installed a wind turbine, and when there was no wind they drove a generator from the steam engine of the threshing set. When that was hired out, they had a gas engine to provide electricity.

61

I asked him if he could remember the Troubles:

'Oh yes. They used to drill over the road in the field there. One of our men, he used to go and join them of an evening or at weekends. The rebels used to dig trenches across the roads into New Ross, and when the army or the Black and Tans wanted to get along they had to put planks over them first. We had eight of the rebels come here one evening and demand a meal. My mother had to feed 'em. What could you do? — you just had to give 'em what they wanted. One night we had a dozen Black and Tans knock on the door – they wanted a meal and to be put up for the night. They slept in the loft, and put an armed sentry at the gate. We'd sent a man in to Ross with the horse and cart to get some iron. He was full of beer coming home, and when the sentry called to him to stop he just kept on coming. My father had to run out and stop the man shooting him. But we had no real Troubles here. Not like Cork and Tipperary and places like that. There was no-one shot and not much damage done.'

One man they employed as some sort of supervisor, though, had been an officer in the British Army. He became very unpopular and people thought he was a spy. He had to leave — in a hurry. 'They were going to shoot him.'

I asked him if there was any fun in his young days. He answered yes. When people at last began to get bicycles ('before that they used to walk into work — three or four miles very often') the younger set would cycle into New Ross every Saturday to go to the pictures. 'There were plays too, and often a pantomime or some such.' There were plays in Whitechurch also — 'sometimes they'd put up a big tent, sometimes they'd use one of our big barns.'

Hurley, the national game, would be played in the field behind the church. 'We'd be out there playing until eleven o'clock at night on fine summer evenings. I played the last game I ever played in 1938. And do you know, not one of the players in that game except me is still alive.'

He remembers a huge concert inside one of their barns, organized in 1917 in aid of the Red Cross. 'I remember the big red crosses hung in all the windows,' he said. Ireland was passing through a strange stage at that time. Irishmen were joining the British Army in their thousands to go and be slaughtered in France, while many of their fellow countrymen were exhorting them to stay at home and fight their real enemy: the colonial power. Who was right, and who was wrong?

But, I thought, as I sat there sipping Harold's whiskey and listening to what was to me a fascinating conversation, wouldn't the kind of local labour-intensive enterprises that the Warren family ran on their farm be the best way to solve Ireland's (or any other country's) unemployment problem? Local initiative — local production to serve local needs — is better than luring in foreign electronics companies with huge grants and long tax exemptions to produce utterly useless high-tech products. (Show me the computer that can grow a sack of spuds!)

But Harold gave me the answer to my unspoken question, the answer in the short term at least. 'My daughter and son-in-law found they had too much work to do last year, with the sheep. They employed a man. It cost them twenty-five pounds a day and he'd come at ten and go at five. I told them to stop it, quick. It would have broken us.' We had both heard on the radio the night before this that a study had found that a man with a wife and four children would be far better off on the dole in Ireland than in a job which paid him £12,000 a year.

Harold Warren is a substantial farmer, owning his own land, and once the partner in a big business. I asked him what he thought of the people who had lived in the big houses round about, the old landlords who had divided up nearly the whole of Ireland, the 'Protestant ascendancy' as they used to be called. I had a feeling he might be on their side, he is, after all, a Protestant:

'Look, it is ten miles from New Ross to Duncannon. On that road there were ten big houses or mansions. They were all surrounded by huge stone walls — I wonder what they paid the poor devils who had to build those? Each one had what I call a "duck house", a little cottage beside the front gate. Some poor old widow-woman would be allowed to live in there and she'd have to come scuttling out every time his lordship was driven out by his chauffeur. And she'd have to be there to bow and scrape and shut the gate when he came back. I thought nothing of those people at all. They were rude and arrogant and no loss now they've gone.'

So much for that. I asked him where he went to school as a boy:

'When I was a very small boy I would have to get up in the morning,

63

milk three cows, then catch the pony and harness him and drive my sister and me into New Ross. We'd go to St Catherine's School there.'

St Catherine's is a small Protestant school, which, like all the other schools, is financed by the government. From everything that I can see, the school system in Ireland is very good indeed. Scholastically, it seems very advanced. Education is taken very seriously in the country, but the pupils seem to me to remain children longer than their counterparts in England. They have a freshness and a spontaneity that delights, and they have no inhibitions with adults.

In 1844 it is recorded that there was a 'hedge school' in Whitechurch. There were such schools all over Ireland, held in somebody's house or cabin. Children paid the teacher, generally with country produce. Surprisingly, much Latin was taught in them. There was a strong tradition of learning Latin in Ireland, going back to pre-Norman times, when an educated man was expected to know it. Brian Friel's brilliant play, *Translations*, set in the West of Ireland in the mid-nineteenth century, deals well with this fact.

Although I cannot find out when our Catholic church was built in Ballykelly, it is known that there was a thatched chapel at Dunganstown (opposite the Kennedy Homestead) in 1743, and that on the visit of Bishop Sweetman to it in 1753 Father James Nolan preached a sermon — in Irish. Although most children are taught Irish at school you never hear them talk it in our area. Some adults take it seriously and try to learn it properly; Angela does, and attends whenever there are lessons in New Ross. But, sadly, in the whole of Leinster, this quarter of Ireland, there are no true Irish speakers who use it in everyday communication. Those who laboured so hard to destroy it succeeded only too well, and those who are trying to revive it seem to labour in vain.

CHAPTER EIGHT

~

A Voyage to Our Town

I F YOU NAVIGATE UPSTREAM from our house, northwards towards the town of *Ros-Mic-Truim* or New Ross, you pass a steeply sloping hill which, once woodland, was cut over recently, but is now tumbling back into forest again. It is called 'the Seven Acres'. Then there is Pat Kennedy's farmhouse, set slightly back from the river, and an area of reclaimed marsh before it. My neighbour, Johnnie Whitty, and Pat Kennedy reclaimed it together, not so many years ago. It is a great place for mushrooms. Then, quite near the river, there is a magical place. Nobody but we river people know anything about it. It is a shooting or hunting 'box' of late Victorian or Edwardian origin I should say, designed rather like a Swiss chalet, empty and deserted, lost in a grove of unkempt bushes and big trees. I am sure there must be a sleeping princess therein, waiting to be awakened by a kiss.

We pass the Pink Rock (to port, or to the west of us) where 5,000-ton cargo ships have to dance a kind of tango to pass in the tortuous channel there. The river bends sharply eastward, and on our starboard hand there is Stokestown House, a Georgian mansion set in fine parkland, which was the heart of a big estate. In 1608 it was the seat of Nicholas Dormer, a Catholic, who was then Justice of the Peace. In 1634 Dormer was returned to parliament for New Ross. In 1642, on 22 June, he was expelled from parliament, along with the other Catholic members, on the grounds of high treason. On 22 May 1657 Nicholas Dormer was exiled to Connaught, and his estate of 500 acres taken from him and granted to Roger Drake.

It may seem strange that a Catholic family could have gone on owning land as late as 1657 in County Wexford, when one reads of the efforts of the Bishop of Ferns (the centre of the diocese) in 1612. In a letter of that year to his archbishop (in Dublin), he says: 'By the Grace of God I am what I am, and by the said Grace assisting me, I will endeavour myself daily more and more to root out Popery and sow the seed of true religion . . .'

In the same letter, he mentions Nicholas Dormer as being one of the 'harbourers of priests' against whom he was going to proceed. But, as R. F. Foster describes in his excellent history *Modern Ireland 1600–1972*, up until the first half of the seventeenth century, most of the land of Ireland was still under Catholic ownership: 'sovereignty, not expropriation, was still the keynote of official policy.'

But Cromwell was to change all that. By an Act of Parliament of 26 September 1653, the 'town of Wexford among other port towns was reserved by the State for satisfying the Adventurers, the Army, the public creditors', and the parliament of England determined to 'clear all the towns of Ireland within their power of their former inhabitants, though English by blood, and people them afresh with English of English birth of England.'

The said Roger Drake, who was later to be given the 500 acres of Stokestown, was one of the 'English of English birth of England', and went to Wexford town as Agent for the Victuallers of the Navy. We read that in 1653 he was given licence to manufacture barrel staves in the town on condition that he employed only 'English and Protestants'. And so it passed that when Nicholas Dormer got kicked out of his estate, Roger Drake was given it; and his descendants still live there, although their name has changed to Stewart, through marriage. Michael Stewart still farms many acres (although by no means all of the original 500) and grows a lot of market garden produce. He farms very intensively and very well. His wife Penny keeps a large flock of turkeys, among other things. The birds run about outside and seem very happy; and one of them makes us happy at Christmas time. Sandra, Michael's sister, lives with her husband Des in a house nearby and is one of the most energetic women I know. For some years she had a caravan on the roadside (on the Kilkenny side of the river but in full view of the family mansion) serving food to lorry drivers, some of whom contacted her on citizens' band radio when they intended to call in. She also does catering for big dinners and other events, and is apparently splendid at it. She is in the process of taking over her mother's flower shop in New Ross, which is a most flourishing business. Des is a skilled mechanic, and has a big workshop in which he repairs motorcars, tractors, farm machinery and anything else anyone cares to bring him.

I describe the goings-on of this family to indicate how very well many of the old 'Protestant ascendancy' families have adapted to the completely new conditions of post-Independence and post-Land Reform Ireland. These people have integrated perfectly with the new society that has grown up around them, and by and large they are extremely popular.

If you live in this country now you find it very difficult even to imagine the Troubles, when misunderstanding and bitterness, between the handful of people who owned all the land and the multitude who owned absolutely nothing at all, shadowed the country. Land Reform was carried out gently and humanely: the landlords were left with whatever land they were farming themselves (that is, that which was not let to tenants); and a fair price was paid for the land that was compulsorily purchased from them to be sold, on a long mortgage, to the tenants. A few of the old landowners moved to England; most of them stayed on in their rambling old houses, often finding it hard just to maintain them without the customary army of servants, gardeners and maintenance men. True, some of them retreated into a world of equestrian concern, in which the horse became almost an object of worship. A few took refuge in a kind of harmless, amiable pottiness. A noble lord I have met, who lives in a mighty castle filled with a king's ransom of art treasures, kisses his wife good-bye every morning, gets into his car, complete with a bottle of whiskey, a glass, and yesterday's London *Times*, drives himself a hundred yards away from the mansion over a lawn, turns the engine off and either listens to the BBC on the car radio, reads the paper, or sips the whiskey. He leads a harmless existence, and I cannot imagine that he will ever have a traffic accident — and, I am told, he has splendid relations with his wife. Another lord I know has converted his mansion into a temple of the Egyptian goddess Isis. It is a sight to see.

But others have grappled head-on with the altered world they find themselves living in, farm such land as is left to them with energy and enthusiasm, and are willing to innovate (the list of IOFGA, the Irish Organic Farmers and Growers Association, contains many of their names). Yet others have gone into business, and entertain paying guests in their mansions, or run courses or other events. Ireland has a vast supply of great mansions (they didn't by any means all get burnt down in the Troubles) and hopefully they will one day play a great part in the life of the nation. They could be centres of art and culture, as no doubt a few of them were in the old days when they were first built. But then it was culture only for the few; now perhaps it could be culture for all those who want it.

But to the oars, for we must fare further up our river. Just past Stokestown House we come to a once-beautiful wood, which has now been substantially destroyed for the accommodation of a mess of cement bulk tanks, grain elevators and the like. There is a floating pontoon in the river, alongside which small coasters draw up to unload their cargoes. The few surviving trees in the wood are beginning to exhibit that grey look that comes from cement dust blowing over them, and no doubt most of them are doomed.

I welcome small port installations such as this, and the small ships carrying cargoes to them, for, after all, small is beautiful in this as in other things, and Ireland is an island and must have sea trade. But industrialization inevitably has its down side, usually in the form of pollution and urbanization. Ireland has, I believe, passed through its stage of anything-goes capitalism. After the Second World War a great wave of industrial prosperity hit the country. Any foreign firm could come here and put up a factory which, because of its polluting nature, would not have been allowed in its own country. Ireland escaped the classical Industrial Revolution but enthusiastically welcomed a sort of high-tech chemical and electronic industrial rat-race after the fact of Independence had finally sunk in. The people left their little farms and country villages and swarmed into the cities, principally Dublin; huge, soulless suburbs boiled out over the surrounding countryside, and I cannot help feeling that they are inhabited by an uprooted people. The rows and rows of industrial housing flung up in the industrial cities of England two hundred years ago must have had the same rootless quality.

I think this demographic movement is over now — it has spent its force. People are even beginning to come back to the country again. Many of the Japanese, American and West German factories put up in such a hurry in the 1960s and '70s have closed down: as things became tighter for the foreign owners at home they tended to close down their far-flung branches first.

There is unemployment here. Emigration is beginning again, and young people are looking towards Australia, England, the USA — some of them, Europe. This may be sad for Ireland, but it is good for the rest of the world. There is a leavening of Celtic blood in all the predominantly white countries of the world, and it does them good. The Welsh, the Scottish Highlanders and Islanders, and the Irish have been flung out world-wide and have stamped their character and qualities — and they have outstanding qualities — on wherever they have gone. What can they know of Ireland who only Ireland know?

But back at home there is a new awareness growing up. The people are beginning to realize that they inhabit the most beautiful country on earth, and they are increasingly determined to do all they can to keep it that way. It is only a beginning but all things have to begin . . .

On, past the cement dust and the ruined woodland, and the river takes a sharp turn left. We begin to see, far ahead, signs of New Ross. It looks a splendid town from the river. To port, on the west bank or Kilkenny side, is a long quay, which almost always has ships tied along it, discharging fertilizer, coal, or other imports, and loading grain for export. But to starboard is the town itself, built along the river bank but spreading up quite a steep hill to heights beyond. Two lofty church spires dominate it, and along the waterfront there are a number of massive stone warehouses, huge blocks of buildings, five or six storeys high. I don't think those that remain will be pulled down now, even though they are underused, as people have woken up to the fact that they are part of a unique heritage and should be preserved. Maybe someone will wake up one day to the fact that they would make damned good warehouses again, even though they are not made of plastic.

The warehouses are interspersed with pubs. We steer our boat alongside one of the flights of stone steps leading up from the river to the quayside; we tie her up and go ashore, and go into one of these pubs. The nearest one to where we are moored will probably be Matty Ryan's. He has renamed it The Mariner's Bar but no local would know what you were talking about unless you used its old name. Mariners frequent it though, for sailors off the ships drift in here. Matty's son-in-law was such a sailor, from the Philippines. Years ago, he sailed into New Ross, fell in love with Mr Ryan's daughter (as who could blame him?) and is, now that his father-in-law has practically retired, the *de facto* landlord — and a very good one too, though the pub is really a husband-and-wife business.

The family owned a fleet of schooners, and Matty has shown me bills of landing for freights of timber that his father's ships used to sail over from Scandinavia and land at New Ross, in front of the pub. Old photographs of the waterfront show it crowded with schooners, and brigantines, and ketches and barges, with horse-drawn carts being loaded or unloaded on the quayside. Then as now, New Ross was a busy port, and today it flourishes exceedingly: over half a million tons of cargo go in and out per annum and ships of 5,500 tons have berthed there. A ten-year dockers' strike in nearby Waterford did New Ross a power of good, though in the past the rivalry between Waterford and Ross led to open warfare.

New Ross may have been new once but it was a long time ago. The first

69

bridge over the River Barrow (which I should guess is well over a quarter of a mile wide at New Ross, with strong, rushing tides) was built to the orders of Earl William, Marshal of England; King John went over it in June 1210. The town was bound to be of importance, both strategic and commercial: firstly because it was at the head of navigation for sea-going ships, secondly because it had the first bridge over the river (and the only one for a long way).

The Vikings may have had a settlement here but it was the first wave of Normans who built New Ross. The pre-conquest Irish were not town people: they were a pastoral race, living in scattered farmsteads and often moving with their flocks and herds up on to higher ground, or out into the extensive peat bogs, in the summer time (the way of life known as *transhumance* in France, and the *hafod* system among the Welsh, who did the same thing). The Vikings were the first people to build true towns: at Dublin, Waterford, Limerick and other places along the coast. But as soon as they could, the Normans set about building castles everywhere, and also strong walled towns.

By 1537 the whole of County Wexford belonged to just three men, and none of them had very Irish names: one of them was the Earl of Shrewsbury, one the Duke of Norfolk and the other Lord Berkely. Certainly none of them lived in Ireland, and they may, indeed, have never even visited it. They didn't have it quite all their own way though. Their tenants and servants went in mortal fear of two families: the Kavanaghs and the MacMurroughs, who constantly harried them and drove away their cattle. Somehow the English just could not drive them out of their forest fastnesses in North Wexford and County Carlow. In 1539, the Council of Ireland, after travelling from Dublin 'publishing the King's injunction, hearing the Word preached, and executing felons', wrote to Thomas Cromwell, the King's secretary, saying:

'The Saturday following we repaired to Rosse, which towne having been heretofore oon of the beste townes in this lande, being also situate in the best place of that part for subdueing of the Kavenaghes, is in manner utterlie decaid and wastid, and so hathe been theis many yeres by reason of the contynuall warr and adnoyance of the Kavenaghes, and the contention betwixt them and Waterford, which cannot be holpen whiles the Kavenaghes remayne onreformed.'

We read in Thomas Darcy McGee's *Life of Art MacMurrough* that, about this time, large numbers of English left County Wexford and migrated back to Pembrokeshire in Wales because of the harassment of the Kavanaghs. Now, Dan Kavanagh runs a very good grocery shop on the crossroad, just along the quay, and is a very peaceful fellow. Indeed, there are a lot of Kavanaghs around, and none that I know of are 'onreformed'.

A little further along the quay from Dan's shop is Richie Roche's Bar. Richie is somewhat larger than life, in more ways than one. He is a very tall fellow, strong with it, with red hair and a flaming red beard. His long narrow bar is the resort primarily of young people, although the odd swinging oldie such as myself does frequent it too. When Angela and I broke down in our car somewhere between Dublin and New Ross, in the middle of the night, Richie was the most obvious man to ring up for help. He left his children to mind the bar, drove out to us immediately, and drove us back to his pub, where we spent the night. What with one thing and another, it was three days before we actually got home, and when we did so, it was in a car lent to us by Richie. Richie it was, too, who drove me to the bone-setter to have my hand repaired. We have had enough adventures with Richie, by and large, to fill a book with the account of them. He often turns up at the end of our quay here with a boatload of kids, and it is like a raid of the Visigoths: they are quite 'onreformed', God bless them.

Somewhere back in Richie's ancestry, there must be a man named Richard Fitzgodebert, who came from Rhos in South Pembrokeshire and, because his castle was built upon a rock, took the name of de la Roche. He was recruited by Dermot MacMurrough when that Irish prince went to Wales to find allies to help him fight against the O'Rourke, and De la Roche was one of the very first Normans to go across. The name became transmuted to Roche, and I know of three Roches, all brothers, who all own pubs on the banks of the River Barrow. Richie is one of them.

But when I state that the pre-conquest Irish were not townspeople, they did have settled places, and many of these were monastic. In what we now call New Ross there was the principal monastery of Saint Abban, who travelled far and wide in Europe and Ireland (he made three pilgrimages to Rome, on one of which he was made a bishop) and established monasteries in various places, including Berkshire. We will meet, incidentally, many other Celtic saints in this book, not only in Ireland but even in the centre of Europe: for much of Europe was re-Christianized by Irish missionaries after the flame of the faith had nearly been extinguished by the barbarian in the early Dark Ages. As for Saint Abban, he died on 27 October 630 AD.

71

New Ross, in the past, had many other important religious foundations, but they were, of course, all destroyed by Henry VIII's creatures. Where the holy Augustinian friars used to sing praises to their God you now hear the bleeping of the electronic cash tills of a supermarket. There is the magnificent Early English-style ruins of the Church of the Canons Regular in Mary Street. Mr Tottenham's fine Georgian mansion up on the hill (the Tottenhams owned the town for a few centuries) has been turned into the Convent of Mercy.

The present town of New Ross was founded by Isabella, the daughter of Strongbow and his Irish wife, whom Strongbow was able to marry as part of his bargain with Dermot MacMurrough. The deal was that if Strongbow (Richard FitzGilbert de Clare, Earl of Pembroke) came over to help Dermot fight against his old enemy Tiernan O'Rourke, he would get a large chunk of territory and also Dermot's lovely daughter: Aoife. The Isabella who built New Ross was the daughter of that marriage.

Because Isabella was closely related to the Irish septs, or tribes, round about — notably the MacMurroughs and the Kavanaghs — she did not even have to build a wall round New Ross: they left the town alone. A hundred years later, though, the burghers found it necessary to fortify their town, and quickly; and there is a splendid description of how they did it, written at the time in Norman-French, by Friar Michael Bernard of Kildare.

On the Feast of the Purification, 2 February 1265, the townspeople went out and marked the line of the wall. It was then decreed that 'on the ensuing Monday, the Vintners, the Mercers, the Merchants, and the Drapers, should go and work at the Fosse, from the hour of prime till noon.' Accordingly they did, and the friar tells us that over a thousand men went out to work every Monday 'with brave banners and great pomp, attended by flutes and tabors.' As soon as the hour of Noon had sounded 'these fine fellows returned home, with their banners borne before them, and the young fellows singing loudly and caroling through the town.' The priests also, who accompanied, 'fell to work at the Fosse, and laboured right well, more so than the others . . . The Mariners, likewise, proceeded in good array to the Fosse, to the number of 600, with a banner before them, on which was depicted a Vessel.'

Every Tuesday, out came the tailors and cloth-workers, the tent-makers, fullers and celers (saddlers). On Wednesday, out came the cordwainers, tanners and butchers 'and they went forth caroling loudly, as the others did'; on Thursday, the fishermen and hucksters. Friday's contingent is illegible in the ballad, but on Saturday out went 'the Carpenters, Blacksmiths and Masons, in number about 350.'

And on Sunday, surprisingly in that day and age, went forth the ladies of the town! And they didn't just stand about and look pretty:

'Know, verily, they were excellent labourers, and they all went forth to cast stones and carry them from the fosse. And whoever had been there had seen many a beautiful woman, many a mantle of scarlet, green, and russet, many a fair folded cloak, and many a gay coloured garment. In all the Countries I have ever visited I never saw so many fair ladies. He should have been in a fortunate hour who might make his choice amongst them.'

Well, there are still plenty of very beautiful ladies in New Ross. And how magnificent if, today, when the town council wishes to carry out some improvement, a new sewage scheme say, the citizens could march out to do it, in their various guilds and bands, 'with brave banners and great pomp, attended by flutes and tabors.' New Ross town council, please note.

Up in Irish Town, on the hill to the east of what used to be called English Town down by the river, you can still see traces of this mighty wall. One gate remains: a gate that was once called Ladies Gate, because it was actually built by the ladies, but later renamed Three Bullet Gate, because Oliver Cromwell fired three cannon balls at it when he attacked the town. Near it is a pub called the Three Bullet Inn, in which I have heard some great singing. And down behind the medieval tower lives Mr Power, who has, or had, until a thoughtless planning decision made him pull it down, a blast furnace in his back garden. He used to cast all sorts of iron objects, and cast for me the pigs of ballast that I have in my sailing boat; a most useful man, in a world where most people seem to get paid big money for making nothing.

Oliver Cromwell did not have to storm the town because the garrison wisely surrendered and lived to fight another day. They were allowed to march out, with their weapons, and the townspeople were promised freedom of conscience — 'provided they did not practise the Popish Mass'. In the 1798 rebellion, the rebels stormed the town and took it, after a violent and bloody battle, but were dislodged again, with great slaughter.

New Ross is a good little town to live near. It is rare that Angela and I need something from the outer world that we cannot get there. Down in

73

Lower Town, which was the old port town along the river, plenty of small shops manage to struggle along, despite competition from the supermarket. The loyalty of their customers, I think, keeps them going. There are, that I can think of, four good butchers, perhaps as many chemists, uncounted pubs, plenty of bookmakers, plenty of Dickensian lawyers inhabiting dusty chambers, and at least half a dozen doctors — one of whom, once a year when I have to renew my driving licence, bangs me on the back, says 'You're as fit as a trout!', signs the bit of paper that I have to present to get my driving licence, and passes me over to the charming girl downstairs who says, 'That'll be ten quid.'

But up the hill, around Irish Town, is where most of the people live. There, there are ancient steep streets, lined with old terrace houses; there are large modern housing estates; there is a great, broad high street, made wide enough to accommodate the hundreds of cattle, horses and sheep that used to be driven up it for sale, for it was the market street. There is one small supermarket up there too, and a few other tiny shops, a big convent and convent school, a small hospital, which people are always trying to close down and then reprieving at the last moment, and a couple of really good pubs.

If you leave the enormous church in Lower Town after Mass on a Sunday and walk along to the New Ross Hotel (the only hotel in the town, an old, traditional building — I should say late Victorian), you can attend the Jazz Session. There are several very good local amateur jazz artists in Ross and they take you right back to the heart of Dixieland — or somewhere like that.

New Ross can stand for scores of small country market towns in Ireland, although not many of course are busy sea ports. It is old and unspoiled, many of its houses from what must have been a very prosperous Georgian age, nearly all its buildings of stone. Ireland is lucky in that the time of its great urban prosperity was during the late eighteenth and early nineteenth centuries: an age of tasteful, large, generous, sensible and truly useful buildings which are as serviceable now as they were when they were new. Dublin, which was certainly the most elegant and civilized-looking city in northern Europe until the end of the Second World War, was badly vandalized by speculators, so-called 'architects', and corrupt politicians. Savage damage was done.

But the small country towns of Ireland have not been so spoiled and are delightful places in which to live or to wander quietly around as a visitor. And if you cannot find good singing, good traditional music, good fellowship and the *craic* in New Ross pubs — that is, if you find the right one — then you will find these things nowhere in the world.

CHAPTER NINE

~

The Boys of Wexford

I
N THE MIDDLE OF NEW ROSS we have the Tolsel, which is a handsome Georgian building now used as the council chambers. Opposite it, in front of Dempsey's Bar, is an heroic statue of a young man holding a pike. And you cannot say anything about County Wexford unless you mention the events commemorated by this statue: 'the 1798 Rebellion', or more commonly 'the '98'.

It might seem at first sight that this rebellion was a simple rising of the Catholic peasantry against the Protestant ascendancy; but it was much more complicated than that. It was, in fact, a spill-over from both the French and the American revolutions. And it was not simply a war between Catholics and Protestants: it was led, in County Wexford in fact, by a Protestant, and many of the militia on the government side were drawn from the Catholic peasantry.

As we have seen, Oliver Cromwell drove all the Catholic landowners, or at least as many as he could catch, over the Shannon on to the wet, windy and barren rocks of Connaught. But former tenants remained, and rented small farms from the new Protestant landowners. They could be turned out at any time and had to compete with each other for farms, which led, of course, to the escalation of penally high rents. Thus the Catholic peasantry was reduced to acute poverty. Cromwell tried hard to exterminate the Catholic Church, killing or transporting any priests that he could lay his hands on. Amazingly, the majority of the people of Ireland clung fast to their religion, and priests lived clandestinely, and celebrated secret Masses in secret places. All over Ireland you will find 'Mass Rocks': isolated rocks which once served as secret altars.

Then, after the defeat of that pusillanimous monarch James II and the subsequent defeat of the Catholic army that he had deserted, at Limerick (it is fabled that when he reached Dublin after fleeing from the Battle of the Boyne and complained that his troops had run away, a lady said to him: 'Well your majesty won the race'!), the persecution of Catholics hardened. Penal laws were introduced, under which no Catholic could stand for parliament, vote, hold any office of state, join the armed forces, carry arms, own a horse worth more than £5, practise at the bar, hold a lease of land for longer than thirty-one years, buy land, or leave land to any of his children — unless one of them happened to be a Protestant, in which case that one must inherit it all. Thus, by 1790, only a fifth of the land of Ireland belonged to Catholics. Catholic parish priests were tolerated, provided they registered with the authorities (who could take away their authorization at will), but no bishops or archbishops were allowed. It was hoped by this provision that the Church would simply die out, because no new priests could be ordained. But young men fled to France, Spain and Italy, and trained for the priesthood there.

It shows some extraordinary persistence, or resilience, of the Catholic Irish people that they did not simply change over to the new religion. They had every incentive to do so, every disincentive to remain true to the old one. No doubt if a majority of them had become Protestants, Ireland would still be under the British Crown. It is interesting that both the Scots and the Welsh adopted different religions to that of the English establishment: the Welsh Methodism, the Scots Presbyterianism; and it is the fact that they refused to accept religious rule from Canterbury that has enabled them to retain whatever independence they still have. I saw as a boy, the defiance of the farmers of East Anglia to both the Anglican Church landlords and the Anglican Church itself, because they clung to the Methodist or Baptist faith. It seems that when a people does not wish to be taken over body and soul by a ruling class some instinct tells them to profess a different religion. We English had our tithe war too.

The eighteenth century was a horrible one for the people of Ireland — although not as bad as the nineteenth, when they had the famines. The rack-rented peasantry struck back at the landlords by forming secret societies: the 'Whiteboys', the 'Defenders', the 'Oakboys' and others. These committed what became known as 'agrarian outrages'. The members of them probably had no great ideas of Irish nationalism; they just wanted to pay fair rents for their farms so that they could live decently and feed their families adequately. They lived in one of the most fertile countries in the world, with a fine climate for growing crops and rearing cattle, and yet they existed in utter destitution. There are scores of descriptions by English and other

77

foreign writers of the dreadful poverty in which most of the country people lived. The greatest of these writers — one of the greatest Englishmen who ever lived in my own opinion — was William Cobbett. In letters home to the people who worked on his farm in Hampshire he wrote such things as this:

'The landlord generally lets his great estate to some *one man*, who lets it out in littles; and this *one man* takes all from the wretched farmer.'

And this, a description of a stock market in Mullinavat:

'There might be 4,000 people; there were about 7 acres of ground covered with cattle (mostly fat), and there were about three thousand beautiful fat hogs . . . our chaise was actually *stopped and blocked by fat hogs*. There was a sight to be seen by me who had never seen thirty such hogs together in the course of my life, these hogs weighed from *ten* to *thirty* score each! Ah! but there arose out of this fine sight reflections that made my blood boil; that the far greater part of those who had bred and fatted these hogs were never to taste one morsel of them, no not even the offal, and had lived *worse* than the hogs, not daring to taste any part of the *meal* used in the fatting of the hogs! the hogs are to be killed, dried and tubbed, and sent out of the country to be sold for money *to be paid to the landowners*, who spend it in London, Bath, Paris, Rome, or some other place of pleasure, while these poor creatures are raising all this food from the land, and are starving themselves.'

Cobbett at least understood the cause of the hunger and poverty, but he did not recommend the right remedy. He believed that the landlords had a perfect right to own all the land and rent it out to the cultivators. He merely pleaded for better poor laws, so that the starving people should get charity. We will have to wait until we get around to the West of Ireland in our travels and stand by the grave of Michael Davitt, the real founder of the Land League, before we find what the remedy was. Thackeray travelled round Ireland at about the same time that Cobbett did, in the early nineteenth century. He wrote an amusing and entertaining book, but he too noticed the awful poverty of the peasants. He put it down to the laziness of the people, but he was not a countryman, and understood little of what he saw. It doesn't matter whether you are lazy or not: if you have no land, no job, and no food, you will starve.

So the rack-rented peasantry formed themselves into secret societies in the mid-eighteenth century to threaten those agents and landlords who were too vicious in their evictions, pulling down cabins and turning people who could not pay their rents out on to the roads to die. Some agents got pitch-forked, some houses got burnt down.

The government reacted by flooding the country with soldiers and armed police, and mercilessly flogging any poor man they even just suspected of being a member of any of the secret societies in order to make him talk, or sing as they say.

I have read descriptions of these floggings made by worthy vicars of the Church of England or doctors, who had to be present at these occasions, that absolutely make the blood run cold. 'I'm a'cuttin' through — I'm a'cuttin' through!' shouted one poor devil, pleading for mercy; and one eyewitness (a parson) complained that, although standing yards away, he was splattered with blood and bits of skin and flesh. Very often the back-bone, kidneys and other internal organs of the victims were exposed to view. Of course if they sang, and told the names of their companions, the flogging stopped and they only got shipped off to Australia — if they lived, which few of them did.

So by the year of the rebellion, 1798, the Catholic peasantry of Wexford, as of other counties, was thoroughly disenchanted with the government of the country. But a new factor emerged that was a backwash of the French and the American revolutions: a new, fairly wealthy, educated and liberal-minded, Protestant middle class had grown up. The members of this social group were also disenchanted with rule from the English government, for they felt they were being taxed unfairly and that trade was being hampered (Ireland was not allowed to trade freely with the world outside Britain). The example of first the American colonists in throwing off the English yoke, and then the French in getting rid of their landed aristocracy, encouraged the professional and trading classes of Ireland to try to do likewise. So the most dangerous yet of the Irish secret societies was founded: the 'United Irishmen', an attempted union of Prods and RCs. Now the last thing that any imperial power wishes to see in any of its colonies is for the subject people to unite. Divide and rule has always been the objective.

So the Dublin government took against the United Irishmen and, with the help of some informers, managed to arrest and hang most of the leaders.

A planned French invasion, with a United Irishman named Wolfe Tone in it, failed to land in Bantry Bay owing, some say, to 'a Protestant wind' which blew the ships back to France but also, perhaps, to the lack of seamanship and lack of resolve of the French officers. The Irish were let down by their allies every time.

So the planned rebellion of the combined forces of the French, the Irish middle classes, and the Irish peasantry, went off at half cock. In County Wexford though, the peasantry did rise, led by the redoubtable Father Murphy, who objected to having his little thatched chapel at Boolavogue, in the parish of Kilcormack, burned by the soldiers. Most of the story is told in P. J. McCormack's ballad:

> In Boolavogue as the sun was setting
> O'er the bright May meadows of Shelmalier,
> A rebel hand set the heather blazing
> To call the neighbours from far and near.
>> Then Father Murphy from old Kilcormack
>> Spurred up the rock with a warning cry.
>> 'Arm arm!' he cried, 'For I've come to lead ye,
>> For Ireland's freedom we'll fight or die!'
>
> He led us on 'gainst the coming soldiers
> And the cowardly yeomen we put to flight.
> T'was at the Harrow the boys of Wexford
> Showed Bookey's regiment how men could fight.
>> Look out for hirelings, King George of England,
>> Search every kingdom where breathes a slave,
>> For Father Murphy of County Wexford
>> Sweeps o'er the land like a mighty wave.
>
> We took Camolin and Enniscorthy,
> And Wexford storming drove out our foes.
> 'Twas at Slieve Coilte our pikes were reeking
> With the crimson blood of the beaten Yeos.
>> At Tubberneery and Ballyellis
>> Full many a Hessian lay in his gore.
>> Ah Father Murphy had aid come over,
>> The Green Flag floated from shore to shore!

At Vinegar Hill o'er the pleasant Slaney
Our heroes vainly stood back to back,
And the Yeos of Tullow took Father Murphy
And burnt his body upon the rack.

    God grant you glory brave Father Murphy
    And open Heaven to all your men.
    The cause that called you may call tomorrow
    In another fight for the Green again!

The 'Yeos' were the yeomanry, Protestant landowners of English extraction who formed mounted infantry units. The 'Hessians' were the mercenary soldiers hired from Germany by George III.

The rebels were initially commanded by a Protestant landowner named Beauchamp Bagnal Harvey, a member of the United Irishmen who had sympathy with the oppressed peasantry. After an abortive attack on New Ross the command was taken over by another Catholic priest, Father Roche. But the rebellion was doomed to failure. The rebels made the mistake of fighting pitched battles. Of course all insurrectionary country people should fight guerrilla warfare — fading away into the countryside, keeping on the move, striking unexpectedly and disappearing again. But how could untutored and unarmed peasant farmers know about things like that? And how could a rabble with pikes face a disciplined army with muskets and cannon with, at the back of it, the greatest empire of the world? After several impressive victories, the rebels made the mistake of digging in on Vinegar Hill (instead of dispersing into the countryside and hiding in the mountains or forests until ready to strike again) and they were signally defeated. And then, of course, the real slaughter began. An estimated 50,000 people were killed by the victorious government army, most of them in cold blood. The floggings started now in real earnest, the half-hangings and pitch-cappings, to extort confessions and obtain the names of fellow rebels.

The government determined to extirpate any traces of Irish or Catholic resistance. But atrocities were not committed on one side only: when the rebels had stormed Wexford town they threw a lot of Protestants off the bridge to drown; and there was a nasty incident when, near Enniscorthy, they imprisoned some people in a barn and set fire to it.

Bagnal Harvey tried hard to prevent this sort of thing, for the whole philosophy of the United Irishmen was to forget sectarian differences and for all Irish people to unite, Protestants and Catholics together, to secure

Irish freedom from English domination. But it was premature. The bitterness that had grown up over the centuries since the Reformation was too entrenched: too strong. The same bitterness that makes apparently ordinary, decent citizens murder each other in Northern Ireland today was what flung the innocent Protestant citizens over the bridge in Wexford town all those years ago. I remember my agnostic brother saying to me one day: 'The trouble with Northern Ireland is that there are two too many religions in it.' What is so sad is that there is only one religion in Ireland really: the actual doctrinal differences between Catholicism and Protestantism are so trivial as not to be worth even a smile. All the bloodshed, and burnings, the Inquisition with its racks and tortures, the pitch-cappings and floggings, the religious wars (which raged all over Europe, not only in Ireland), and the butchering of women and children was about nothing, nothing at all, no doctrinal or philosophical or religious issue worth more than a yawn. There is only one religion in Ireland of the slightest importance in the North or the South, and since the mission of Saint Patrick there has only ever been one — Christianity, the religion of peace.

Enniscorthy is just one of many towns to bear the scars of sectarian difference. A splendid little market town and old river port on the banks of the River Slaney, it is at the head of navigation of that river, and small sailing barges, called Slaney gabards, used to carry the produce of the countryside down the river to the seaport of Wexford for shipment to England. There is a fine Norman castle in the middle of the town which is now a museum, and a very interesting one too. Besides many 'by-gones' of great interest, there is a room devoted to the '98 rebellion. (Enniscorthy was captured and looted by the rebels on that occasion, and just to the west of the town stands Vinegar Hill where the rebels were finally defeated.) And there is also a big collection of mementoes of a much later rebellion: that of 1916. Enniscorthy was one of the few places outside the centre of Dublin to be taken over in that year and declared to be a republic: a republic which lasted only a very few days. The rebels after that war were not pitch-capped, or half-hanged, or flogged until their kidneys showed: they were simply taken to Kilmainham Jail in Dublin and shot. There are their rosaries and lockets and other personal possessions, and last notes to their mothers and loved ones, on show in glass cases in the museum; and the other day — Easter 1991, as I write this — there were great celebrations in Enniscorthy in their honour, for it is the 75th anniversary of their deaths. Their fight too, like that of the men of '98, was apparently fruitless. But was it? If a subject people keeps on fighting long enough, if enough blood is spilt and enough guilt is felt by the conquerors, then they sometimes get their independence.

And here I feel I must make my own position clear in all this. How can I, as an Englishman, take the side of Irish rebels against the English Crown? Well, I am not an Englishman (although I would quite like to be one). I was born in England, yes, but to paraphrase the old Duke of Wellington, being born in a stable does not make you a horse. My father was pure Scottish, my mother was almost pure Welsh (she had no English blood), but I was brought up in England and schooled in English schools. I steeped myself in English literature and culture and tradition, worked in the British colonial service in Africa (and I still believe that most Africans were far better off under it than they are now under their military dictators) and served for six years in the British army — in the British colonial army in fact, as an officer in the King's African Rifles. I am proud of all this.

But I will always side, everywhere and every time, with small nations that are oppressed by big ones. I will always side with ethnic groups trying to get their freedom from the bullying ruling nations. The great evil of our world is lust for power and territorial aggrandizement. I left Wales, after seventeen years of living and farming there — the happiest years of my life — because I could not forgive the Welsh people for rejecting their chance of devolution in the referendum that the colonial power allowed them to hold. I would love to see, I would be prepared to fight for, a free and independant Wales — and Scotland, Brittany, Basque country, Nagaland, Kalistan, Kurdistan, Tibet, and any other small nation, anywhere in the world, which has been absorbed by, and is being oppressed by, a big one. It is not small countries that destabilize the world, it is big countries. Since Independence, Ireland has destabilized nobody. The only role the Irish army plays is in the peace-keeping forces of the United Nations. Ireland is a threat to nobody.

Now the charge might be levelled against any writer who drags up stories of torture and atrocities — those, for example, committed by the English military authorities against the rebel Irish — that such descriptions only perpetuate hatred and bitterness, that they keep old animosities, far better forgotten, alive. But I do not think you can rewrite history or suppress the truth just in order not to inflame people. You have got to have it all out in the open and then try to urge forgiveness and peace. The Irish people, most of them, have got their independence now. And the old United Irishmen would be delighted, if they came back here, to see that we really are united now:

there is no discrimination, no hard feeling, left. The six counties of Ulster could join the other thirty-six tomorrow and they would find a true and friendly welcome; and they would discover that this is a fine country to be a citizen of. The law is the same here for RCs and Prods, Jews and Muslims, Hindus and Hare Krishnas. A band of Hare Krishnas came through New Ross the other day, shaking begging bowls, and good Catholic citizens were running out to give them money. I asked one later why she did it, and she said: 'Well, if they didn't need it they wouldn't be asking for it.'

And what I have frequently said to my more Anglophobe friends in Ireland (and there are a few — although they are kindness itself to individual Anglos), when they talk about the atrocities committed in the past by the English in Ireland, is: 'Well they were doing that too in England.' There were penal laws against English Catholics too, and I have seen many a 'priest hole' in ancient English houses, where persecuted priests used to be hidden from the soldiers. There was many a peasant rising in England too, always ruthlessly put down by the government forces, often with the help of foreign mercenary troops. We had our hangings, and our floggings, and the English had — and still have, unlike the Irish — a disgusting system of land ownership, whereby ninety per cent of the land is owned by just two per cent of the population. After Kett's peasant rebellion in Norfolk in 1549, the Earl of Warwick, who was in command of the forces that suppressed it, suddenly became alarmed at the thousands of hangings, and said: 'Is there no place for pardon? Shall we hold the plough ourselves, and harrow our own lands?'

No, the issues have never been divided black and white between the Irish and the English. It has been far more complicated than that.

CHAPTER TEN

~

The Raiding Party

AT ABOUT NOON ON A RAW WINTER DAY of 1982, on an otherwise completely deserted shore of North Pembrokeshire, in West Wales, three men stand gazing out to sea. They say little. When one of them does utter a few words, he speaks with a strong German accent.

What they are seeking finally appear: a great motor-ship rounding Strumble Head, heading across Fishguard Bay. Without saying a word to each other, except a muttered 'There she iss,' from the German, they turn away and climb into a waiting minibus.

Earlier that day, at Rosslare Harbour across the Irish Sea, another scene had been enacted. Three somewhat old and battered motor vehicles had been driven into the car park and out of them had got six men and two females. Several of the men carried strange-shaped packages in their hands. There are short greetings between them and then one of their number — obviously the leader — says, 'Your man hasn't turn up.'

But just at that moment a fourth car, also old and battered, comes into the car park, its engine making a cacophonous sound. Out of it get a beautiful young girl and a strange old man with spectacles and a tweed cap which conceals the bald front to his head but completely fails to control the unruly gingery-grey curls sticking out at the back. Any watching police agent would have been immediately suspicious of his appearance. In fact there is an air of conspiracy about the whole lot of them; they look like men and women steeled for some desperate adventure.

The two last-comers walk over to the rest of the group and short greetings are exchanged. Then the old gingery man addresses the oldest of the others. 'Well, Captain, shall we go aboard?' The man thus addressed mutters an order and the whole group begin to file off in the direction of the waiting ferry.

85

I am the man with the greying gingery curls, the last driver to arrive; Angela is the beautiful young girl with me. How we became caught up, inextricably, in these events can be explained, although not simply. The circumstances are peculiar. There is one thing certain: we cannot get out of it now. We are the virtual prisoners of the rest of the party.

Silently we file aboard the great ferry ship. We are lucky. Nobody searches the strange packages some of our members carry. We make our way to the bar. We all sit down around two tables that we have dragged together. People are eyeing us curiously. There is a feeling of tension. The bar is not yet open.

The ship sails, the bar does open and our tables are rapidly filled with pints of stout and little nip bottles of Powers whiskey.

'Right,' says the old man addressed as Captain. 'Shall we give it a go?'

He picks up the case he has been carrying, which looks strangely like a violin case. He opens it and pulls out ... a violin. At least it looks like a violin — it might have been a Thompson sub-machine-gun in disguise. But no, it is not. He plucks at it and begins to get it into tune, and you cannot do that with a Thompson sub-machine-gun.

The big man with the white moustache pulls a clutch of mouth organs out of his pockets. The lady with the piled-up hair produces a pair of spoons. A sinister-looking young man with a black beard pulls a melodion, or button accordion, out of its case. Another young man produces a set of *uileann* pipes, and another uncovers a *bodhrán*. They all begin to play, and the drumming adds a certain atavistic spice to the music. The other passengers relax and seem to be enjoying it. They have been lulled into a false sense of security.

The members of our party — our Raiding Party, for that is what it is — seem to be able to play and drink at one and the same time. In fact Jim Smith — 'Captain' Smith, our leader — is the only man I have met who can play the violin, smoke a cigarette, eat a sandwich and drink a pint of Guinness all at once, simultaneously. True, the crumbs from the sandwich and the ashes from the cigarette do tend to end up inside the violin, but this does not in any way detract from the dulcet tones issuing from it.

Now I must leap backwards in time again to describe how the whole improbable affair of that first Raiding Party came about. We were sitting in Bob Roche's Bar in Duncannon, in County Wexford, many many years after my first visit to that place in the governess car. Bob's is my favourite bar. Eileen, the lovely landlady, will, during the herring season, bring you a fresh herring wrapped up in silver foil to roast over the hot coals of the fire. On the night in question there had been music. But, by the small hours, music had given way to talk, and someone was discussing the great raid of the Normans, under their leader Strongbow, when they sailed away from Pembroke to land at Baginbun, just a few miles from where we were. They knew that I came from Pembrokeshire and that is what started them off on the subject.

'Isn't it time you went and had your revenge?' asked Angela, 'You Wexford men?'

'What do you mean?' asked Bob. 'Put Fishguard to the fire and the sword?'

'No, worse than that,' said Angela. 'Go and play music to them.'

And so the great idea of the Duncannon Raiding Parties was born. There were three Raiding Parties to Pembrokeshire, and on the third so many people tried to crush into the pub that the situation got out of control and the police had to be called. The fourth Raid struck right into the heart of Europe, but that I shall describe in due course.

Now, how Captain Smith received his commissioned rank was like this. Some days after the night I have been describing, Angela and I walked into Bob's Bar with the laudable intention of quenching our thirsts. Most of the members of the intended Raiding Party were there. An ominous silence fell as we walked in.

I walked over to Bob. 'What's the trouble?' I asked, out of the corner of my mouth.

'John, this thing could get out of hand,' he growled.

My heart fell. I supposed the whole thing was over. I was beginning to find, like many another roadie before me no doubt, that handling a bunch of musicians is like treading among egg shells, or rather, anti-personnel mines.

'The trouble is,' Bob went on, 'they're after arguing who's coming and who's not. Half the population wants to come.'

'Right,' I said, and turning to the party at large I addressed them, rather as Strongbow must have addressed his cavalry before the battle of Baginbun. 'Jim,' I said. 'You are henceforth to be Captain Smith. You are Captain of the Raiding Party. You will decide who's coming, and who's not coming. And nobody is going to argue with you. Any questions?'

There were no questions at all, and everybody seemed quite satisfied with this completely democratic decision. There was no further argument, and everybody was contented except, I suppose, those unfortunates who failed to find favour in the Captain's eyes, or ears.

As for those on the receiving end of the Raids — the defending forces, as it were — I happened to be good friends with the three landlords of a pub called the Sailor's Safety, in Pembrokeshire. The Safety, as its habitués call it, is one of the most splendidly sited pubs in the world. It is at the bottom of a long, steep lane, so narrow it has passing places only, right at the edge of the sea, at a place called Pwlch Gwaelod. Here is a magnificent little sandy bay, with rock cliffs flanking it and a splendid view across Fishguard Harbour. Small ships could lie at anchor in the bay, if there were not a north-west wind blowing, and many a time I have beached there in a sailing coble.

Now why were there three landlords? Well, officially and legally no doubt, there was only one: Robin, a gent from the City who was inordinately fond of the works of Rudyard Kipling. We habitués knew this and used to turn it to our advantage. For when we wanted to go on drinking late, which we invariably did for the 'crack' was good there, and, say about two or three in the morning, Robin was trying to kick us out, we would just have to say: 'Robin, give us a blast of "Gunga Din".' And he would. And barrack-room ballad would give way to barrack-room ballad until the break of day, and the beer would flow.

But the other two-thirds of this composite landlord were: Chris, an enormous, quite young, man from Birmingham with a Brummie accent you could cut with a knife; and Rainer, an equally enormous man, from Germany, with a goatee beard. How he had strayed to that place, why he was there, I never really found out. But all three had hearts of gold, and a more delightful pub to be in there never was (with the possible exception of the pub described in Belloc's *Four Men*, the Inn at Bramber — but maybe that was only a myth).

So, after the idea of the Raiding Party had been mooted, I went into this pub and addressed the Three. 'Do you like Irish music?' I asked. The answer was a strong affirmative.

'Tell you what, old boy,' said Robin, after I had explained. 'We've got a big mobile home out there, and a chalet. We'll put you all up and feed you and beer you, for nothing. How's that?' Well, as far as I was concerned, that was that. Certainly a better reception than Strongbow and his warriors got at Baginbun.

So we must go back to the Sealink Ferry carrying the Raiders across the Irish Sea. Some person of genius (I think it was Paddy) twigged that it was silly buying little nip bottles from the bar when we could get litres from the duty-free shop.

The music, like the drinking, was fast and furious. People came and joined us and songs were sung. And although both before and since that voyage, I have done that crossing so many times that I have paid for that ferry, I have never enjoyed the crossing more.

But I was worried. 'They'll peak too early,' I said to Angela. 'By the time we reach the Safety they'll be burnt out.' I little knew my men.

The ship docked but the music went on. The table was by now entirely covered with empty litre bottles. Plastic bags filled with bottles newly bought from the duty-free shop seemed to cover the floor. 'At that price ye feel it's a sin not to be takin' yer allowance,' said Paddy, sagely.

So eventually the instruments were put away, the clanking bags of bottles gathered up and, with Angela shepherding us all rather like a sheep-dog controlling recalcitrant sheep, we filed down the gangway. We were met by the three lordly landlords of the Sailor's Safety, in a large van. They had to take us in two loads. Angela stayed with the second load, and she began to wonder just what she had taken on. Arrive at the pub, though, we eventually did. And did the Raiders take a rest? No, they did not. They called for a bottle of whiskey, pulled out their instruments and began to play again as lively as ever. True enough, Andy Monahan, the man of the big belly and the splendid moustache who played the mouth organ so magnificently, didn't he go outside and lay himself down on a table in the yard and sink into slumber? When we saw him, somebody shouted for four candles, one to be placed at each corner of him, and he awoke to find himself being measured with a tape measure somebody had thought to bring, as if for his coffin.

The word seemed to be getting around and people began to drift in to the pub, Welsh people living in the surrounding countryside. And they loved it! They had all heard Irish music on the radio, for on that coast you get a better reception of the Irish radio than of the English, but they had never actually encountered Irish musicians in the flesh before.

The Welsh are choral singers of the finest calibre. Their own folk song tradition, now being painstakingly revived again, was wiped out by the Methodist revolution. Their instrumental music went with it, except for the harmoniums in the chapels. The most magnificent hymns were a product of Methodism, but music as a thing to bring *joy*, or sheer *fun*, became a lost concept. Some of the greatest singers in the world are Welsh but they almost never get the chance to sing solo. As soon as a person begins to sing, all the others join in, as if by compulsion, until you get the fine, swelling harmonies

89

that you have to live in Wales and be welcomed into Welsh farmhouses to hear.

But it was obvious that the people drifting into the Sailor's Safety, were astounded at what they were hearing. And suddenly, they found that they could dance. Dancing, like secular song, was completely suppressed by the Methodists. But this music made you dance. (When it is played at a wake one is amazed that the corpse does not leap up and join in!) Soon the whole pub was dancing. The spirit of the dancers transmitted itself to the musicians, and the one worked upon the other: the violins went mad, the skirl of the pipes joined them, and then that most marvellous of instruments, the tin whistle (it is astonishing that such sophisticated music can be wrung out of such a simple device!) and the barbaric rattle of the *bodhrán* all combined to lift the hearts of the most stolid.

Being so far from anywhere, the Safety is seldom troubled by the police. The neighbours never complain, because there are no neighbours. The fun went on fast and furious most of the night. Then people began to draw away out of sheer exhaustion. But not the Raiders. When the last of the customers left they seemed to be just getting into their stride. Jim Smith was seventy on that first Raid (he is seventy-eight now, God bless him). Andy was retired, having been a farm worker all his life, and he and his wife Bridie had managed to rear up a fine family of ten children on an Irish farm worker's wages. And so they had a stamina denied to lesser men. (Someone asked Captain Smith on the Salzburg Raid why he was so fit, and he answered: 'Plenty of hardship!') And our three brilliant landlords seemed to be in no hurry to get to bed. They knocked us up a fine supper, the Welsh and Irish national anthems were played, and we fell to and ate. It was five o'clock in the morning.

I woke up at nine. I was amazed, almost appalled, to hear — no, it couldn't be, it *couldn't* be, but it was! — music! I crawled out of bed and took myself round into the bar. There, sitting round a table on which stood a litre bottle of Bushmills whiskey, sat the entire group. 'What happened to ye? You're after oversleepin',' complained Paddy, the caretaker of the great fort of Duncannon, who seemed to be tucking in to an alcoholic breakfast.

But Rainer and Chris came to the rescue. 'Br—e—a—kfast!' they bawled. And there were ten plates piled high with eggs (multiple eggs), bacon (rashers and rashers of it), fried bread, baked beans, tomatoes, etc., etc. People staggered to the table and fell to. Not so Paddy, of the fine white beard. 'I'll be contentin' meself with the Bushmills,' he said.

'No you vill not,' said Rainer. And he moved up behind Paddy's chair, put his arms under Paddy's shoulders and hauled that character to his feet. (One can almost talk of brute force!) He more or less frog-marched Paddy to his chair, thrust him down in it, and said: 'Now eat. You vill eat — every bit!' And Paddy ate every bit, and was the better man for it.

Most of us did manage to struggle up the steep path on Dinas Island after breakfast, though we were back in time for the midday session of course. At least one of us had a snooze that afternoon(!). But the evening and the night-time sessions were more frenetic than the night before. On the third night, things were almost beginning to get out of hand. Too many people were trying to crowd in. But in the event all was well — just.

And then came the time to sound the retreat; the Raiders had got to make their way back to their ship. But we did just look in at Bessie's on the way to the ferry (well, not precisely on the way to the ferry — Bessie's is a fine pub in the middle of the Gwaun Valley), and more music was played, and more beer was drunk; and I only got them out by virtue of a great sailing ship's foghorn, or bull-roarer, that one of my sons-in-law had given me. It is a huge brass cylinder with a piston in it, and makes a noise that can be heard for ten miles on a foggy night. And passing through Fishguard, didn't they all dive into the Fishguard Arms? The foghorn had to be used there, too, with desperation. When we finally got to the ferry, the crew had to lower the gangway again to let us on: they were already casting off the mooring lines.

The foghorn now hangs on the wall behind Bob's Bar, a trophy of the Raid. Maybe I will arrange for it to be put among my grave goods when I die. Perhaps I can blast my way into Heaven with it. I don't suppose I shall get in any other way.

CHAPTER ELEVEN

~~

The Salzburg Raid

'I T'S MOVING. IT'S MOVING!' complained Jim Smith, standing back and waving his violin case. He was referring to the escalator at the brand new terminal building at Rosslare Harbour. We were about to board the ferry for Fishguard, and subsequently to fly to Austria. Angela coped, as usual, with the crisis. Jim was safely got on — and off — the moving stairs, we boarded the ship, found the bar, and there was music all the way across the sea. People got up and started leaping about and dancing, but nothing got out of hand, and we landed and (a thing I shall never do again) we crowded into a bus. It was, to me, an ordeal on wheels (it was the Muzak I could not stand). It drove all through the night and eventually tipped us out at Victoria bus station at some horrible hour in the morning. If there is a hell it is probably very like Victoria bus station at some hellish hour in the morning. After some bacon and eggs we took another bus to Heathrow, where we boarded a plane. I sat near Bridie, my favourite lady, and she loved the experience of flying. She couldn't get over it.

We had to change planes at Frankfurt and there Angela's troubles really began. There were twelve of us — it was a big Raid. Angela played the part of sheep-dog but the rest of us, alas, did not play the part of obedient sheep. There were duty-free bars; there were duty-free liquor shops; there were strange exotic goods on display. Frankfurt airport is a huge, rambling, confusing place. Angela and I knew this, the rest of them did not. We had only a limited time to get off the first aeroplane and on to the second. We only just made it.

We had Richie Roche with us, you see, and there is nothing at all sheep-like about him. And we had a man, a flautist, of great stature (he played an enormous wooden flute), whom Richie quickly gave the name of the Big Cat. Richie, the Big Cat, and, I have to admit, the writer, were off to a bar. By sheer force of character Angela got us all together again, and aboard. And we forged on, through the skies, to the land of our intended depradations.

At Salzburg airport we were met by two perfectly beautiful girls: Heidi, whose eyes were as blue as the clear skies above the Alps on a summer day, and Anita. Even to look into Anita's eyes would reduce a strong man to jelly. The Big Cat immediately fell hopelessly in love with her. Each girl (students doing holiday jobs) drove a minibus. We crowded into these and were driven off in the direction of Salzburg city.

A few of us were much-travelled; some had never in their lives left County Wexford. We had a hard core, of course, of veterans of the old Raids into Pembrokeshire, and these gave a stiffening to the enterprise. But I could not help putting myself in the place of those who had never seen a mountain before, nor a city, nor a house of over three storeys, as we drove into that superb and ancient town, and through it, to our hotel.

This was, of course, built of wood, in the splendid architectural style of the Alps. We found our rooms, and then, when all assembled in the big lounge with the bar in it, Heidi (who, it appeared, was the senior of our two drivers, interpreters, philosophers and guides) said to us: 'Order anything you like at the bar — but you do not pay. The government pays.' We could scarcely believe our ears. Most of us, of course, took this as a reason to be moderate in our demands but not the Big Cat. Oh no, not the Big Cat!

We were served a meal of Byzantine sumptuousness, and then we played. I didn't play, of course, being only the roadie. The Big Cat played, though, thus demonstrating that he could play as well drunk as he could sober. (My mother once wrote a reference for a lady companion who applied for a job as matron in a very respectable public school. She ended it by saying, 'Julia is a fine driver — drunk or sober.')

We were a strong force. Besides our Captain, Jim Smith, who was in great form although in his eighties, we had our beautiful Liz Cassidy, née King, and her two charming little daughters: Åna, seven, and Sínead, fourteen. Åna is a great little dancer and, of course, the darling and mascot of us all. Sínead is a dancer too and an accomplished musician. She plays several instruments including that very rare and difficult one, the concertina. Then there was Andy Monahan, a veteran of many Raids, and Bridie, his lady, playing the spoons and the *bodhrán*. There were two teenage boys, nephews of Liz, who made up a foursome for set dancing with Liz and Sínead. There was the Big Cat, all seven feet of him; there was Richie Roche, who was, in the language of the pop world, a groupie (he didn't play anything although he does give a great vocal rendering of 'Nancy Spain'); there was Angela; there was me.

After food we played, and sang, and danced. The locals loved it, and stayed up several hours past their normal bedtime (the Austrians are a dreadfully hard-working race). We stayed up long after that, and when I finally crawled out of bed the next morning (or rather, the same morning) it was to find the Big Cat, sitting by the bar and already heavily into the beer, which he found to his taste. But we were soon whisked off, after *frühstück* of course, by our two beautiful guides and drivers, into the mountains.

Salzburg is not just a city of course: it is a country too. The city is merely the capital of a large stretch of country, mostly mountains, and some of the most splendid scenery on earth. Every night, for the next week or ten days, we would be driven to some superbly beautiful village and housed in an hotel, where we would play music until the small hours to the most appreciative audiences. But it was not just a one-way cultural exchange: often there were local musicians, or dancers, or singers. The contrast between them and our boys and girls was great. The defending side played very carefully, very skilfully, and always with printed music in front of them; they played things like zithers and harps. Our lads never had printed music — they played by ear. (Few, if any, of them could read music.) They played as if they were born to play and had played all their lives. The Austrian music was beautiful, civilized, Mozartian, but somewhat predictable. The Irish music was wild, varied, often impassioned, played with immense verve and skill, and never predictable. We were just not a predictable lot. And the least predictable of us was the Big Cat.

On about the third day we were to perform in a village which was having an 'Irish Week'. The Salzburgians are besotted with Irish music. We played in the streets, we played in the bank, and in the evening we were to play in a large theatre.

Now the Cat could hold his beer — oh yes, he could hold his beer. But he was taken to heart by a German brass band (one of those *oompa-oompa* ensembles so beloved of the Austrians). He went off with them and I think they showed him an altogether different standard of beer drinking to what he had known before. They all had huge bellies, as big as the enormous brass instruments that they were staggering along under. He's met his match, I thought. And, thinking of the extremely formal and sober nature of the impending occasion in the theatre, I was quite glad that my man had found new friends. We have seen the last of him for the night, I thought.

And it was indeed a formal occasion. It was a big theatre, packed, and up on the stage were no less than four groups of musicians: three of them Austrian and one, our lot, Irish. The Austrians looked very, well, genteel. In the audience, next to me, was Alfred Winter. Freddie Winter is an old friend of Angela's and mine, and by way of being a Minister of Culture, of sorts, for the Salzburg government, the fairy godfather of this particular Raid. He had invited me several times to go and speak at various seminars, conferences; one ceremony, the Presentation of the Salzburg Golden Ring to a famous son of Salzburg, I had to say the *laudatio*. It was Freddie who had invited us all over on this occasion as well. And there were many other dignitaries at that theatre: it was a grand, almost a state, occasion.

The proceedings were opened by two trumpeters dressed in magnificent uniforms, who came to the edge of the stage and blew a mighty fanfare, which nearly raised the roof. Now, because they were aiming their trumpets straight down the wide aisle which ran down the middle of the auditorium, they gave the impression that they were blowing the fanfare for some expected honoured guest — some monarch perhaps, or maybe the Angel Gabriel himself.

One naturally turned one's head to look down the aisle, to see if this was indeed the case. The splendid, huge, ornate double doors at the end were flung open with a mighty crash — and, yes, no, not a visiting monarch, not the Angel Gabriel, but the Big Cat walked in. Nearly seven feet tall, huge with it, he looked a splendid figure, waving his flute in one hand and his shirt in the other. All eyes, of course, had turned to look at him. He stood there, apocalyptic, until the trumpets were stilled, then advanced, unsteadily, weaving from side to side, up the aisle of that splendid theatre. He teetered as though he would have fallen backwards but somebody, with great presence of mind, put a chair behind him and he subsided into it. He put his flute to his lips, thought better of it, and just sat.

But the show had to go on. A lady, a folky-looking lady — the equivalent of some worthy member of the English Folk Song and Dance Society — came to the edge of the stage. Her grey hair was tied up at the back of her head in a neat bun. She began to talk. She talked in German of course, and no doubt very learnedly, and at great length.

The Cat got so that he'd had enough of it. He waved his flute

95

and shouted, 'Enough of the talk! Let's have some bloody music.'

Freddie leaned over to me. 'John,' he said. 'You've got to do something.'

I got up, went over to your man, and said, 'Come on. We're going to go and have a drink.'

He followed me like a lamb, but when we got outside I didn't really know what to do with him — he stood in the middle of the road and held up the traffic. But who should come to my rescue but the lovely Anita. And where all my efforts to tame that mighty fellow had failed, one look of those doe-like eyes succeeded: the Cat was tamed; he ate out of her hand. She led him off, and we had no further trouble that night. Next day, the Big Cat was driven to the airport. He had decided to go home.

One day we drove high, high up into the mountains. We went to the highest inn in the *Lande* of Salzburg. It was a cloudy day, but occasionally we got glimpses of soaring, snow-clad peaks, quite unlike the little rounded hills we get in County Wexford. We drove right up above the snow line, and the less dignified of us had a great game of snowballs. Inside the inn we were greeted by two splendid men wearing full Tyrolean regalia, who pushed in two huge alpenhorns. They were far too big to carry and had to be shoved along the floor. Facing each other they made these extraordinary instruments bellow and groan. Then our lads broke into 'The Blackthorn Stick'.

Our hosts seemed as interested in entertaining us as listening to us entertaining them. They took us to see great castles; they took us to old-fashioned farmsteads in the mountains, where farmers and their wives still make good cheese and butter, and feed their cows on real hay, not some mucky silage. We had to keep an eye on Tom Dunne because of his inordinate love of tractors. Tom Dunne, besides being the finest Irish fiddler I know, is a tractor mechanic. Whenever he saw one in the mountains (and the Austrians have many and strange ones) he would leave the party and rush off to look at it, to crawl underneath it, to photograph it. You expected him to make love to it, except that I suspect he was already in love — with the doe-eyed Anita.

One evening, after the usual late-night session, Tom, Jim, Angela and I sat out on a balcony looking at the splendid stars above the mountains. The mountains were clad in fir trees there, and the house we were in was, of course, entirely made of timber. The night was beautiful.

'Tom,' I said. 'That must be a fine violin you've got. I've never heard a fiddle with such a glorious tone.'

'Do you know what,' he said, 'it's all this timber. The buildings are all wood. We're surrounded by wood. My violin feels at home; she responds to it; she feels this is where she belongs.' Tom is not only a good tractor mechanic, and a fine musician, he is also a poet.

Then came the day when we were to perform before the *Landeshauptmann*, who is the President of Salzburg *Lande*, and an ex-President of Austria itself, no less. The venue was an ancient monastery in the middle of Salzburg city, a place I was quite familiar with already. The monks have their own brewery and run their own pub, a very good one (your holy monk makes your finest landlord), and we were to perform ensconced in this bar.

The night before, we had all been guests of various private people, and Angela and I had been in the house of some very hospitable Austrians who had a Turkish friend. The young Turk, who was a sporting sort of lad, announced his wish to come to the auspicious occasion next day. But when we got to the monastery he was refused entry — it was a private function; you had to be invited. Being an experienced roadie by now, I managed to get him in. I gave him an impressive-looking card to flash and told him just to mumble 'press'. He did, and in he got.

A hefty monk staggered in with a kilderkin of ale and dumped it on the table. Another religious banged a spigot into it with a big wooden mallet and proceeded to draw the beer into beautiful earthenware beer mugs (I still have mine, for they gave us each one as a memento — the monks run a pottery too). The beer was delicious. We found no difficulty in emptying the mugs, and they were rapidly filled again. Music was played; we all shook hands with the President and the ex-President; a fine time was being had by one and all. Suddenly I was aware that my young Turk was waving an empty mug. Alas, nobody was filling it. Not to be denied, he got up, went to the kilderkin, and turned the tap on. Rapidly his mug was filled, and he tried to turn it off again.

But a beer tap doesn't work like an ordinary tap. To turn it off you only give it a half-turn — if you turn it any more it comes on again. My Turk kept turning and turning, and the beer gushed all over him, and all over the polished floor, in a great flood. I knew perfectly well how to turn it off, but for some time I was incapable of doing so — I was paralysed with laughter.

Our hosts the monks were not a bit put out. They were rolling about laughing too, and took the small disaster extremely well. Their beer was evidently musical beer for the music proceeded to get wild and furious, with the inevitable result that people began to dance. The dancers were slithering about on the beer-wet floor, but everybody seemed to think it was very funny and nobody minded at all.

Indeed, the people of the Salzburg *Lande* were uniformly hospitable and kind to us. Although they are citizens of Austria too, I believe they look upon their real country as Salzburg, and it is my experience that the smaller a country is the nicer the people are. And the people we met were the nicest possible; they could not have been kinder to us.

But the high point of the Raid — and the high point of the lives of some of us — was when we were driven out, one morning, not into the great mountains as usual, but over a green and fertile plain. Most of us were farming people, and we took a great interest in the farming landscape as we went. Eventually we came to a steep-sided, conical hill, and on top of it was an ancient church. This, we were told, was the Church of Saint Bridget, and Bridget was, of course, a saint of Ireland. A small crowd stood about on the hillside, all dressed in their best, looking as if they were awaiting the arrival of some great personage if not the Second Coming itself.

A shortish, roundish man, with dark hair and bushy eyebrows, came up to me and said, in English but with a thick German accent, 'Hello. I am Count O'Donnell, *The* O'Donnell'. I nearly said that I was *The* John Seymour but I forebore, because 'The' is a title in Ireland, as it is, or used to be, in Scotland. He meant he was the head of the O'Donnell clan.

'I am one of the Wild Geese,' he said. 'It is seven generations since my ancestors left Ireland.'

The Wild Geese were the old Gaelic nobility of Ireland who, at various stages in the conquest of that country by the English, left the country, with their armies and retainers, and served under foreign monarchs. The O'Donnells, apparently, had eventually found their way to Austria and, after serving in the armies of the Austro-Hungarian Empire, had been granted a huge tract of land, which the man I was talking to still owns. A young, slim, very Irish-looking man came up and The O'Donnell introduced him to me as his son.

But just at that juncture, what we had all apparently been waiting for, turned up, in the shape of a huge bus. I had expected something else from the air of expectancy of the people: a golden chariot, perhaps, swooping down from the sky, attended by a host of angels. But no, a bus. Out of it got a splendid man dressed in an Irish kilt and all the correct accoutrements. He carried a set of bagpipes — not the small-pipes, or *uileann* pipes, that we were used to, but the full war pipes — and he proceeded to play them with great vigour, no doubt startling the eagles on many a mountain crag.

Then, out of the same bus, emerged a figure, a large and well-rounded figure — familiar to all those of us who were from Ireland, from having seen pictures in the papers — a figure in full cardinal's regalia crowned by a red cardinal's hat: Cardinal O'Fiach, no less, Cardinal of all Ireland, to Irish Catholics scarcely less than the Holy Father himself. He was followed by a bus-load of weary and travel-stained pilgrims, sixty of them, making a tour of the shrines of the army of Irish saints, who had re-Christianized Europe after it had sunk into the confusion of the Dark Ages.

But the Cardinal didn't look travel-weary. He seemed hale and hearty and had a merry twinkle in his eye, so our Raiders played and danced for him. He shook hands with us all, then led us into the church and proceeded to celebrate Mass in three languages, in all of which he was equally fluent: Irish, German and English, they were all the same to him. After this we all trooped over the road to a huge inn. The sixty pilgrims all sat down at a long table, and we sat down together at a smaller one. I asked one of the lady pilgrims what part of Ireland she came from and she answered, 'Oh, we all come from the Black North.'

Now the mayor of the village had thought it hospitable to provide each one of us with a glass of schnapps, and these were glinting on the tables when we came in like so many large diamonds. We of the Raid quickly tossed ours back, and then one of the pilgrims walked over to our table carrying sixty more glasses — they had made a vow of abstinence for the pilgrimage! Even we were a little daunted by the task before us, but we manfully — and womanfully — rose to the occasion!

Now Bridie was of the opinion that if you kissed a cardinal's ring you got ten years' remission of your term in purgatory. I cannot imagine that lady going anywhere else when she leaves this world but straight to the highest spot in Heaven, but Angela decided to indulge her. She got up and walked over to the table where his Grace was being entertained by the Mayor, a couple of bishops and other local dignatories.

'I'm sorry,' she said. 'But I don't know how to address you.'

'Call me what ye like, my dear,' said his Grace, taking her hand in both of his.

'We have a lady in our party,' said Angela, 'and she's a poet. She would love to recite one of her poems to you.'

'I'll be right over,' he said.

And over he came. We made room for him at our table opposite Bridie, who grabbed his hand and kissed his ring not once but several times. Then she recited her poem 'Memories of the Past':

There was an old woman named Mary the Coc;
I remember her well when we lived in Lough.
She wore a red hat and only one sock,
And that's how we christened her Mary the Coc.

Now Mary the Coc had no fixed abode,
And when she was young she took to the road.
She was fond of the bottle and fond of the drop,
And Mary was often seen around Lough.

Now Mary the Coc was sure to be seen
When me father, God rest him, was making poteen.
'Yera, Johnnie', she'd say, 'will you sell me a drop?
Sure 'twould help me old chest and 'twould soften me cough.

And me father would say, 'Good heavens, Mary, I don't make it for sale.
If I did I'd be liable to six months in jail!
But sure, now that you're here I'll give you a sup,
But for God's sake be careful, it is very strong stuff.'

Then Mary would glance at the worm in the still,
Saying, 'God bless you, Johnnie, I certainly will.'
And me father would fill up a glass to the top,
And Mary would drink the whole bloody lot!

I remember one night by the light of the moon,
When Mary was sipping poteen from a spoon,
She staggered around and she couldn't keep still,
And she fell on her arse at the top of the hill.

Well poor Mary is dead now, I'm sorry to say,
But I remember her well to this very day.
And if you're out any night after twelve o'clock,
Ah, you'll sure see the ghost of Mary the Coc.

Then me father was caught and was taken to court,
And there was people there from the Barney Fort.
And the judge said, 'Stand up, John, and I'll let you go free —
If you promise to make a wee bottle for me.'

A few nights after that, sure me Dad heard a knock,
And he thought for a moment 'twas Mary the Coc.
But when he opened the door, sure he just couldn't budge,
'Cause standing outside was the bald-headed judge.

'Mr Bennett,' he said, 'I don't wish to be mean,
But I've come to collect me wee drop of poteen.'
And me Dad said, 'Come in, Sir, for I don't begrudge;
What's fit for a king is fit for a judge.'

Well my Dad's in heaven now, and last night in my dream
He was teaching St Peter how to make the poteen.
And sure, Jesus himself even tasted a drop,
And then brought me father way up to the top.

And just 'fore I woke and opened my eyes
He was presenting me Dad with the Nobel Prize.
Now I'm finished my story and I've told you the lot,
So I bid you good night and have a sweet dream —
But beware of the Guards if you're making poteen.

At first the Cardinal seemed a little taken aback by it, but then he relaxed and thoroughly enjoyed it. Jim Smith seemed to get on very well with the Cardinal, as indeed did Andy Monahan. They both knew that he had been a student in Wexford town and they started talking about the county.

'Sing us "Boolavogue"!' urged Jim.

'I'll sing ye the first two verses and the last one,' said his Grace, rather as if he was announcing the hymn to be sung in his cathedral. 'But ye must join in with me, mind.' He had a mighty voice, and together we made the rafters ring.

I am reminded of a story about Edward Fitzgerald — not the one who got shot by the British for leading the United Irishmen in 1798 but the one who translated Omar Khayam's *Rubayat* and lived at Boulge, in my old home county of Suffolk. Apparently, he was with a group of people once, and they

101

were boring him to death with accounts of the number of lords they knew. Old Fitz got up and walked to the door. He turned to the company and said, in a sad voice, 'I knew a lord once.' Then, just as he walked out, 'But he's dead now.'

Well, I knew a cardinal once. Thomas O'Fiach died last year, to the great sadness and distress of us all, for in Ireland he was much loved.

PART THREE

WE GO WEST

CHAPTER TWELVE

Westward Ho!

THE MAN WHO STAYS in one parish for his entire life and really gets to understand it may learn more about the world than the restless fellow who never stays still. But nevertheless, Angela and I, after having spent ten years more or less confined to our own corner of County Wexford, decided to explore further into the island to see if we could penetrate a little deeper into the mystery of that enigmatic land.

We had a small trailer-caravan, and we hitched this to the back of our Lada car and lurched up our rough track. We stopped and reported to Mary Whitty (for it is well for one's neighbours to know when one is going away), drove to New Ross, over the great bridge over our river, and headed for the town of Waterford. To get to Waterford you have to cross the River Suir, which joins the Barrow at Cheek Point. The people of Waterford have managed to get the world to call the great natural harbour where these two rivers meet 'Waterford Harbour'. The people of New Ross would no doubt have liked to have had it called 'Ross Harbour', but that was not to be. Waterford was the busier port of the two but, as I have mentioned before, its business was almost completely killed by a ten-year strike. It is now the main Irish port for Bell Container ships (which don't need dockers, just one crane man).

Waterford is a fine town, and has everything in it that a sensible person could desire. It has an old-world seaport atmosphere. And it is a very old seaport: the Vikings founded it in the ninth century. In the twelfth century, Strongbow, the great Norman leader, sailed past the headland of Baginbun, in County Wexford, as it is now, and which was then occupied by a beleaguered Norman advance guard under a fine leader named Raymond, and landed at Passage East. Giraldus Cambrensis tells us that Strongbow's force was a thousand men, and that he had a fair wind from Milford Haven whence he sailed. On seeing Strongbow's ships pass, Raymond immediately broke out of his stronghold, marched his forces to the Barrow, somehow got across, and joined Strongbow in attacking Waterford.

The city was occupied by combined Danes (or Vikings) and Irish, and well fortified. The first two attacks that Strongbow and Raymond made on the town were repulsed, but then Raymond achieved a breach in the wall through which the Normans, as Giraldus tells us, 'entered manfully ... rushed into the town and, slaughtering the citizens in heaps along the streets, gained a very bloody victory.'

There is a fine round tower at the eastern end of Quay Street called Reginald's Tower. In this, apparently, two Norse earls, both named Sitric, another Norseman named Reginald, and an Irishman named O'Faolain took refuge. The two Sitrics were killed, but Dermot MacMurrough, the Irish prince who had invited the Normans to Ireland in the first place to help defeat Ruairi O'Connor, the self-styled High King of Ireland, arrived just in time to plead for the lives of O'Faolain and Reginald, and they were spared. The town finally fell on 25 August 1170.

If the Irish had been united they could have easily driven out the tiny force of Normans, but then they would not have been the Irish. Ireland at that time still had a Bronze Age culture: the same sort of social and military arrangements perhaps as the Homeric Greeks. The Normans, although of Norse extraction, had acquired in France the disciplines and social cohesion of the Roman Empire. Militarily they were unbeatable because they used the stirrup which made their mounted knights the equivalent of the modern battle tank. They also had an entirely different attitude from other people to the ownership of land.

In pre-Norman Ireland, as in the old Scottish Highlands, there was no concept of personal land ownership. The clan, sept, or other enlarged family group, under its chief, controlled an area of land (by custom usually, but in the last resort by force of arms), and the members of the clan took what land they needed, or what their chief or headman thought proper, to plough and grow their food on. The cattle and sheep were herded over the rest of it, which was common grazing.

The Normans, however, had quite different ideas. After they had conquered a country, huge tracts of land were allotted to the various lords and barons who had helped conquer it as personal, private possessions, and the new owner could do anything he liked with it, or the people on it. The Norman custom of primogeniture ensured that the huge estates thus created should not be broken up, and in fact in England, Scotland and Wales they exist, intact, to the present day. Of course, the lord did not farm himself. He let the land to tenants, who farmed it for him and paid nearly their whole crop as rent. They were allowed to keep just exactly enough to stay alive, for a dead tenant is no good to anybody.

The English, who were most thoroughly conquered by the Normans, accepted this system completely, and the average Englishman could imagine no other, nor can today. They imposed it on all the countries they conquered during the days of the British Empire. So it was in India, where the tax collectors, or *zamindars*, who collected taxes from the free peasants to support the court of the local rajah, were given the land over which they collected the taxes as their own private property by the British, and ever since have acted in the worst tradition of rapacious landownership. The extreme poverty of the Indian *ryot*, or peasant, is entirely due to this mistake on the part of the British Raj. When the English conquered the Scottish Highlands they made the same blunder, and gave the clan lands to the clan chieftains, who promptly began to rack-rent. This successfully drove people off their ancestral lands in the direction of Australia or America, enabling the new lairds to run sheep over the land and thus make money, on which they could go to London and Bath and become imitation Englishmen. The Highlands were devastated and depopulated, and remain so to the present day. As one veteran of Waterloo said to his laird as he embarked for a life of exile in Nova Scotia, 'Ye'll no hae men to fight for ye. Ye'd better train the sheep.'

Well, Strongbow proceeded to the (Viking) city of Dublin, and took that, before returning to our area (the south-east) which he began to carve up into huge estates. Now that he had married into an Irish family he began to take part in Irish internal affairs, and no doubt he and his descendants would have gone on to adopt Irish ways completely. But Henry II, King of England (as well as of much of France), heard of Strongbow's success and decided to go to Ireland himself and get his own slice of the pie. Strongbow went to England to submit to him, and Henry generously gave him the whole of Leinster (a quarter of Ireland, the best quarter), although the legality of giving what you have never had may seem questionable. (Henry had never even seen Leinster.) Henry thereupon sailed for Ireland with a huge army, and made a triumphal progress, giving the various kingdoms to the Irish chiefs who submitted to him, who must have thought that they were being given their own land! He calmly gave the city of Dublin to a group of Bristol adventurers, the original inhabitants having been slaughtered or having fled.

107

Henry sailed back to England from the port of Wexford on Easter Monday 1172 to do penance at Canterbury for the murder of Thomas à Becket.

But as we have seen, the first Norman and Flemish invaders 'went native'. They fell in love with the Irish way of life, the language, the music, the girls. Who wouldn't? They coexisted happily with the old Irish aristocracy, became part of it in fact, and if only England could have left the country alone its history would have been much happier.

But this is not a history book. Angela and I continued our own progress, through Waterford, to Tramore, by the sea — *Tra* is Irish for beach (compare *traeth* in Welsh), *mhor* for large (Welsh *mor*). We drew into a camping sight from where we could see the Metal Man. This looks rather weird: the figure of a man, high up on a stone pillar, rather like Nelson on his column, and dressed as a sailor of the early nineteenth century. We walked to it, wondering what it was, and found that it was on a headland, looking out to sea, with a big wide bay to the east. The next headland had two stone pillars on it equal to the one on which our Man stood. The whole thing was a mystery, and we determined to solve it. So we walked back along the shore of the great bay and came to a tiny artificial fishing harbour. We climbed down the cliff to look at the few boats in it — small half-deckers and some plastic lunch-box pleasure boats — and then climbed up again to find a rather beautiful and distinguished-looking grey-haired lady sitting on a seat there. She had a little dog with her.

We got talking to her, and she told us that the little pier down below (which looked a perilous little shelter in bad weather) was once called Gleann a Chuain, but the name was changed to Lady Elizabeth's Cove to please the wife of one of the Lords Doneraile, the local squires. People now called it simply Lady's Cove. It was washed away in 1883 and the new pier was opened in 1907. She told us a strange story of the bathing customs of Tramore when she was a girl. Nobody bathed in the sea before the First of June because the sea-fairies inhabited the ocean up to that date. Then, on Michaelmas Day, the local children would carry a large doll made out of seaweed, called the *Breedeen*, from house to house, and it was lucky to give them money (lucky for them at least). The doll was then flung out to sea, and nobody bathed in the sea after that until the next First of June.

It seemed most unlikely that our old lady-friend's interests should include anything so outlandish as the Metal Man, but nevertheless it turned out that she was the 'custodian' of that gentleman. Her family (a fishing family) was the oldest family in her area and it was its privilege to care for the strange metal sailor on top of the pillar: it was an hereditary right. The pillar had been built there and the Man set on top of it by a public-spirited local landlord, Lord Doneraile, early in the nineteenth century, to warn ships not to come into the bay. It was a dangerous bay, and many a ship became embayed there. Probably thinking they were sailing into Waterford Harbour, crews sailed in there instead and, not being able to beat out the south-westerly or southerly wind, were driven on to the great sand bar that cuts off the inside of the bay. The Metal Man was there to warn them (indeed he points his arm in a most warning way), and is supposed to be saying, the old lady told us: Keep out good ships, keep out from me / For I am the rock of Misery! He does have his less sombre side, though: if a virgin hops round his column three times on one leg, she will be married within the year.

We drove inland to visit an ogham stone which was marked on the map. After map-reading our way through winding country lanes we found where it ought to have been and I knocked on the door of a bungalow. A boy came out and told me it had been carted away, but he directed us to the Giant's Grave, which he thought would do us instead. We drove to a most remote and lonely place — or at least we thought it was until we suddenly saw an enormous intensive pig farm, an obscene place, down in a valley with a bulldozer working on the hillside. Behind the bulldozer was a pile of great rocks, which we looked at, took a photograph of, and wondered what to make of.

Many learned books have been written about the megalithic monuments of Ireland, Wales, Brittany and other Atlantic seaboard countries, but you can read all these works and still be little the wiser about them. All that is really known is that they were built between about 4000 BC and 2000 BC by Neolithic, or New Stone Age, people, who were farmers as well as pastoralists and hunters; that human bones have been found in many of them, sometimes burnt but sometimes not; that many contain grave goods (stone arrow heads and other implements, and crude pots); that they were respected for quite a long time (in some cases carbon dating has showed up improvements to monuments that were built 1,000 years earlier); that there are a lot of them (1,450 have been recorded in Ireland alone); and that the building of many of them must have been an enormous labour. The capstone (the huge rock hoisted on top of some vertical rocks) on a monument near Carlow has been estimated to be 100 tons. How Stone-Age people hoisted up a 100-ton rock remains a mystery. Maybe some playful millionaire should

get a hundred archaeology enthusiasts together and see if the same thing could
be done today.

Modern people believe them to be the burial places of many pre-historical
heroes, gods and goddesses, and sometimes even fairies or devils. There are
also many tumuli about Ireland, also of great age, and these are supposed to
be the abode of fairies or Little People. It is bad luck to plough over them
or bulldoze them down. It is also bad luck to take iron on to them: the
fairy people do not like iron. (I always leave my pocket knife behind when
I go on to one.) Can it be that when iron was invented, the Bronze-Age and
Stone-Age people feared it, realizing that it was a threat to them, and that
these pre-Iron-Age peoples, who refused to enter the Iron Age, somehow
became translated by popular mythology into fairy people? I wonder. The
only way to get a proper answer is to walk to one on a moonlit night, and
spend the night there, alone. You may hear the voices of your ancestors.

Tramore is a pleasant little seaside resort, with miles of sandy beach backed
by sand dunes and an enclosed lagoon. There are all the appurtenances of a
very popular seaside resort: it is a sort of mini-Blackpool. We walked to the
end of the beach, climbed on the dunes, and walked back along the lagoon
which was rich in wading birds. Huge fossilized trees have been found below
the sandy beach.

The next day, we hitched up the caravan and headed west, along the
road that follows a magnificent coast of cliffs, beaches and rocks, until we
came to a place named Clonea Beech, which has a caravan park. This was
hard by the small seaport of Dungarvan (Dun Garbhan) into which we walked.

When Oliver Cromwell marched into Dungarvan, we are told, a lady
named Mrs Nagle ran out into the street and proffered him some beer.
Puritan though he may have been, he drank it, and it so pleased him that
he decided not to sack the town — although he did of course burn down
the parish church of St Mary's and the Augustinian abbey. But Mrs Nagle is
remembered, by a small, select number of us, in a strange but fitting way.

With pub beer at over £1.50 a pint we indigent and indignant settlers
are constrained to brew our own beer. If we have not got suitable buildings
in which to do this, we do not brew from the raw malt itself, but from malt
extract which we (somewhat decadently perhaps) buy in tins. Now some
genius in Dungarvan has concocted an extract of such distinction, which
makes a beer of such quality, that the likes of Angela and me will drive
miles to get it. With it we make the most splendid brew, and have to warn
our friends and those unaccustomed to its potent strength. It is called *Mrs*

Nagle's Beer. But even Cromwell's Ironsides or pitch-capping would not drag from me the whereabouts of the shop wherein we get it; for if we were to divulge this, and too many good men and true, Puritan or no, resorted there, the price would go up and the quality would come down.

Dungarvan is inside a splendid bay, approached from the sea by a rather sinuous channel through sands, one of which has the ominous name of the Dead Man. It was an early seaport; a carved bone, of the Hiberno-Viking period found in a nearby cave and dated to the ninth or tenth century is evidence of early activity. Saint Gavan is said to have founded an abbey there in the seventh century, but he is not in my dictionary of saints. The Normans soon discovered the bay and as they liked good natural harbours, built a walled town and a castle there. In the thirteenth century, an Augustinian priory was established (the one that Cromwell destroyed), and the lord of Dungarvan had a little back garden in the countryside behind the town that extended over 200,000 acres. Centuries later, the Dukes of Devonshire inherited this little property (God knows what they had done to deserve it, or what it had to do with Devonshire), and during the nineteenth century the fifth and sixth earls pulled down the old medieval town and built what we see today. It is a distinguished little town: their graces made a good job (though with the rents from 200,000 acres it could not have been so difficult).

Dungarvan, like most Irish towns, has had its share of sieges, pillages and plunderings. In 1641 the town opted for the Catholic Confederacy, and was stormed and taken, most of it burned, by Lord Inchiquin. His lordship killed the priests and most of the leading citizens. The Confederacy retook the town and killed and plundered most of the English and Protestants. The Catholics sent ships to France and Spain for munitions. (The only hope the Irish ever had of beating the English was to get arms and ammunition from abroad, for Ireland was not an industrial country and could not produce these things for itself.) But the imported arms were not enough, and when Inchiquin stormed the town again in May 1647 with 3,000 men, it fell to him again. After this, however, Inchiquin changed sides and joined the Royalist cause (the English Royalist cause of course), joining forces with Ormond. The latter, and his army, were defeated at the Battle of Rathmines, just south of Dublin, and when Oliver Cromwell came over himself all effective resistance had ended. He had it all his own way.

The little town fell on hard times after all this, and a nineteenth-century writer was able to report that 'popular feeling held it in derision, passing travellers laughed or blushed at its indelicacies, and industry and trade forsook its fisheries and trades and left its population to conflict hopelessly with poverty as with filth.'

The Dukes of Devonshire changed all this (although it must be admitted that it was under their ownership that it had sunk to that condition in the first place) with their redevelopment of the town. Apologists for English rule in Ireland always say: look how well this or that English landowner built this or that building, industry or town. The Irish nationalist answer to this is: yes, but we, if left to ourselves, would have done it equally well, if not better. The English landowners spent only a fraction of the wealth they received from their Irish rents actually in Ireland: nine-tenths of it went back to England, where most of them lived!

Dungarvan Harbour, or bay, debouches to the east, and the bay is bounded to the south by a peninsular of higher ground ending in Helvick Head. This peninsular is called the Ring, and is unusual. It is a *gaeltacht*, where the chief language spoken is Irish. Further west, we were to encounter many Irish-speaking areas, but the Ring is completely isolated, maybe sixty or seventy miles from the nearest native Irish speaker. It is hard to see how this pocket of Irish-as-a-first-language-speakers has survived, as the Ring is not a particularly remote or cut-off place. We drove there in the car, and gave a young man a lift to his home near Mine Head. On our way we passed a small house which had been garishly and sumptuously painted all over, like a Sicilian cart. To my rather childish taste it looked beautiful. 'We call him Michelangelo who lives there,' said our hitch-hiker. But he knew no more about him. We left him at his home and drove round the coast to Ringville, or Ring village, which has a large modern college where people go to learn the Irish language. It was vacation time and the college was deserted. We found a pub with a sign on it which said 'Music'. We went in, but there was no music. We drove further east and found another pub that did not say music — and in it we found music. There were men with accordions, a lady with a fiddle, and a young boy with a *bodhrán*. We felt at home and happy, as I always do when I hear spontaneous country music, anywhere in the world.

Now I have heard folk music played and sung in many parts of India, in Ceylon (both north and south), in Burma, and in a dozen countries of Africa. I have heard much of what very few Europeans realize exists: the ancient songs and *vastraps*, or jigs, of the Cape Malays, the hereditary deep-sea fishermen of Cape Town. They brought Malay folk music from their homeland in the seventeenth century when they were brought to the Cape as slaves by the Dutch. They picked up the songs of their masters, which they still sing, not in Afrikaans, which is the modern tongue there, but in the old seventeenth-century Dutch of the Netherlands. I have sought out and heard what little true folk music exists in half a dozen countries of western Europe. But I will state with complete conviction that there is no vernacular music, anywhere, to come near the best of Irish country music. If it does not lift your heart and make you joyous then there is no hope for you. But, to back my own judgement up, I must quote from someone who really knew about music. After having complained about the lack of skills in the arts and science of the Irish people, this writer went on to say:

'It is only in the case of music ... that I find any commendable diligence in this people. They seem to me to be incomparably more skilled in [this] than any other people I have seen. The movement is not, as in the British instrument to which we are accustomed, slow and easy, but rather quick and lively, while at the same time the melody is sweet and pleasant. It is remarkable how in spite of the great speed of the fingers, the musical proportion is maintained. The melody is kept perfect and full, with unimpaired art through everything — through quivering measures and the involved use of several instruments — with a rapidity that charms, a rhythmic pattern that is varied, and a concord achieved through elements discordant. They harmonize at intervals by the octave and the fifth, but they always begin with B flat and with B flat they end so that everything may be rounded with sweetness of charming sonority. They glide so subtly from one mode to another, and the grace notes so freely sport with such abandon and bewitching charm around the steadier tone of the heavier sound, that the perfection of their art seems to lie in concealing it, as if it were better for being hidden, an art revealed brings shame. Hence it happens that the very things that afford unspeakable delight in the minds of those who have a fine perception and can penetrate carefully to the secrets of the art, *bore*, rather than delight, those who have no such perception — who look without seeing, and hear without being able to understand. When the audience is unsympathetic they succeed only in causing boredom with what appears to be but confused and disordered noise.'

Now the above was written, not by a modern music critic in one of the more rarified monthlies, but by Geraldus Cambrensis, in the twelfth century! Giraldus despised the Irish (he was one of the first conquering

113

Normans to invade that island, after all). But, obviously, he fell in love with their music. The Irish that he encountered were a semi-nomadic pastoral people so they could not cultivate the sedentary arts such as architecture, sculpture or painting. But the arts that they could cultivate they did, and these were what I would call the 'portable arts': poetry, the oral tradition and music. They had far more, and more sophisticated, poetry than either the Normans or the English (as, indeed, the Welsh did too). They have kept their music, very little of it written down but handed on by ear from one generation to the next, and thank God there are still enough people of real taste in Ireland to give it the support and appreciation it needs to keep going. The young go through a stage of liking nothing but heavy metal, punk and other such ephemeral fads, but most of them find their way back to their own tradition when they grow up (and get more sense). Some of the older people who think of themselves as oh-so-sophisticated affect to despise it. They will go to the Wexford Opera Festival and sit through some opera by Benjamin Britten pretending that they are enjoying it but actually stifling their yawns, yet they will ignore the fine, lively musical tradition of their own country. They are those who, in the words of old Gerald the Welshman, can only 'look without seeing, and hear without being able to understand'.

CHAPTER THIRTEEN

Sir Walter Raleigh
and All That

WHILE WE WERE TOWING OUR CARAVAN through Dungarvan and when we were just coming to the bridge crossing the river there, the tow-bar on our car most embarrassingly collapsed. We were transformed in an instant into a total road block, and as it was a Sunday, and there was some holiday traffic, we became an intolerable bloody nuisance.

Having driven a car and often pulled a caravan over a great part of the British Isles and western Europe, I naturally expected a chorus of frantic and furious hootings and honkings, and shouts of abuse from outraged motorists. However there was nothing of the kind. Drivers immediately jumped out of their cars and ran up to see if they could help. And they actually did help, unhitching our collapsed caravan, dragging it to the roadside, and then engaging in a lively discussion as to where we could find a garage open on a Sunday. Only when all this had been arranged did these people get back into their cars and continue about their businesses.

We took the road to Youghal, but made a diversion south to Ardmore to see the fifth-century oratory built by Saint Declan, who founded his monastery there. It was a beautiful, hot October day when we got there. The place is now a small seaside resort, and we parked our car beside an amusement park, with amusement park-type music blaring out and swings and roundabouts, and lots of happy young children — which I am sure Saint Declan would have been pleased to see. We walked through an almost preternaturally neat and tidy little town to find Declan's oratory: an impressive though very small stone building (impressive because of its great age) and looked at the south-east corner of it where the saint's mortal remains are said to lie.

Nearby is the roofless ruin of a substantial cathedral which, built mostly in the twelfth century, was dedicated to Saint Brendan. We were struck immediately by the fine reliefs on its west front and discovered later that one of them represents the conversion of the Chief of the Deisi, the tribe that inhabited eastern County Waterford when the Normans came. Inside the ruined building are two ogham stones. We had an ogham stone built into the church of Nevern, near my old home in Wales. That particular one is interesting because it has an inscription in ogham on it with a translation of it in Latin. It therefore proved the key to the deciphering of the ogham alphabet. Ogham is a peculiarly Irish phenomenon, an ancient alphabetical writing system of lines set perpendicular to or at an angle to another long straight line. The letters thus formed (something like a petrified morse code) generally spell out funerary inscriptions in the Latin translations. There are hundreds of ogham stones in Ireland and a tiny scattering of them in Wales and West Scotland.

We walked down an extremely tidy, well-kept and attractive little main street (practically the only street in fact) to the seashore, and stood admiring the garden in front of what had once been the lifeboat house but which was now a domestic dwelling. A lady came out and told us proudly that Ardmore had won the first prize three times running for Waterford in the Tidy Villages Competition. We walked along a narrow cliff path, running along the face of a steep cliff, and came to a ruined religious building: obviously part of the ancient monastery founded by Saint Declan.

Some men in a small boat were hauling in a large drift net, made no doubt of monofilament which is completely illegal but used countrywide in Ireland for catching salmon. We sat in the sun and watched them with field glasses, and they caught not one fish. I remembered, many years before I moved to Ireland, visiting Kinsale, not far west of Ardmore, and seeing a group of men hauling in a purse-seine net, and beaching at least twenty great fat salmon. I live on a salmon river and know all about salmon, and I am sad to say that the salmon is well on the way to extinction. It seems as if almost nothing can save it now. As for that beautiful fish the sea trout, it looks as if it is already almost extinct. As far as I can ascertain, not one was caught in Ireland last year as I write this (1991). The reason for it, I think, is quite simply overfishing. There are too many large boats shooting too much monofilament drift net (up to ten or twelve miles of it) off the coasts of western and southern Ireland. The nets are illegal anyway, being monofilament, but they are also nearly always twice the depth in the water than the law allows. Huge piles of these nets are to be seen piled up on the quays of most Irish fishing harbours, yet no action is ever taken against the owners. My friends down at Duncannon, Ballyhack, and over the river at Passage East and Cheek Point, fish quite legally, with legal nets and in the legal season, and one of them told me the other day that he could not even make the price of a drink. More often than not he spends all day fishing and catches . . . nothing.

The only thing that could save the mighty salmon — this great bounty of Nature which used, for millennia, to harvest the richness of the deep seas and bring it back up our rivers to our very doorsteps — is to put a complete ban on open-sea fishing for salmon, and sea trout too. This ban could be backed up by a fleet of gun boats which, if necessary, should use their guns. At present there is open defiance of fishery protection vessels. It is easy to blame the fishermen, but what can they do? Their wives expect them to earn a living and if they catch fewer fish their rivals will simply catch more so they will not be helping the salmon in any way. Vast fortunes have been made by drift-netting for salmon off the Irish coast in the last couple of decades, but the fishermen are killing the goose that used to lay the golden eggs.

So, with these sombre reflections, we strolled back, on that lovely day, along the steep cliff face beside the sparkling ocean, and met an old man who told us that in his youth 'patterns' were held every year here on Saint Declan's feast day, but that these had since been discontinued. A 'pattern' is a saying of prayers over the graves of the dead, and hundreds of people would gather there to hear Mass said and the Rosary recited.

There is a yearly pattern held at a holy place on our own River Barrow, which we can get to by boat. This is Saint Mullins, where there is a holy well, and a thorn tree which is decorated at the appropriate time of the year with strips of rag. Many hundreds, if not thousands, of people assemble there that day; some of them wade through the stream that carries the water away from the well; a Mass is said and the Rosary recited. The one pub at Saint Mullins does a roaring trade.

Youghal (from *cochaill*, meaning yew wood) is a splendid little port town, squeezed between a cliff and the great bay whereon it is sited, with a town wall running along the top of the cliff. The little town, which is a beautiful and fascinating place at the mouth of one of the most beautiful rivers in Ireland, the Blackwater, was originally founded by the Fitzgeralds. Descendants of the lovely Welsh princess Nesta, after the first Norman invasion of Ireland, they conquered and held a huge tract of country in Munster, the south-west corner of the island. They became Earls of Desmond and a power equal to that of the central government in Dublin Castle itself.

We wound through the town's narrow streets with our caravan and headed south-west across marshes, and across the Dissour River. We left the caravan at a site near Knockadoon Head, and went back into the town to have a look round it. The most notable building in the ancient main street is the Clock Tower which straddles the street. This was built soon after 1770 as a prison and jailer's house, and felons (which meant at that time chiefly Irish people) used to be hanged from its windows, as a warning to the rest of the population. Youghal was, like most other Irish towns in the eighteenth century, an almost exclusively English and Protestant town. Such Irish people as did live there could not be 'freemen', and were constrained to live outside the walls. The walls, for most of the town's history, were kept in a good state of repair, for Youghal was a most important place. It was a natural port of entry for Spanish or French shipping, and the Blackwater Valley made a corridor into a most fertile hinterland.

During the Elizabethan wars, when the English determined to put an end to all Irish resistance in Ireland, the Earl of Desmond (a Fitzgerald) took the side of the Irish (his family had, after all, been living in the country for four hundred years by then) and was declared a traitor by Queen Elizabeth. Desmond promptly stormed Youghal, which offered no resistance, and when he was subsequently beaten, the mayor of the town, a man by the name of Coppinger, was hanged by the Earl of Ormonde outside his own front door for failing to keep him out.

An unknown English captain of the army, Walter Raleigh, played a big part in the defeat of Desmond and the Fitzgerald dynasty; as a reward, he was given the town of Youghal and 42,000 acres of the Desmond estate. There is a fine Elizabethan private house, still lived in, next to the great collegiate church of Saint Mary's. This was Raleigh's house, called Myrtle Grove, where he spent much of his time. It was here that he is supposed to have first planted the potato, the plant that was to prove such a snare and a delusion to the Irish people.

Raleigh very soon set about planting his huge estate with English colonists as well: all from his native West Country in England. And he also set about felling the huge oak forests that covered that part of Ireland to turn them into barrel staves. He exported so many barrel staves from his estates to England that the English coopers protested, and said the trade was putting them out of business. More significantly, he completely denuded the country of trees.

The Elizabethan settlers, to whom a vast part of the land of Ireland was given after the Elizabethan wars, were a pretty ruthless lot. Edmund Spenser, the author of *The Faerie Queene*, about the defeated enemy (written, incidentally, in part at Raleigh's house in Youghal) wrote after one campaign that he had taken part in:

'They were brought to such wretchedness as that any stony heart would have rued the same. Out of every corner of the woods and glens they came creeping forth upon their hands, for their legs would not bear them. They looked anatomies of death, they spake like ghosts crying out of their graves.'

But one gathers from the rest of the text that Spenser did not have any real pity, he was simply rejoicing in the success of the military campaign and its very thorough scorched earth policy.

The Elizabethan wars succeeded in breaking Irish resistance almost entirely. Huge numbers of English settlers were imported into the country and given vast estates. They were different from the Irish not only in language, race, and customs, but also in religion. For some reason or other the Irish just would not give up their loyalty to the old faith. Even the so-called Old English, the Irish descendants of the first Norman conquerors, would not give up their faith. And so the seeds of enmity between the Irish and their English conquerors were sown in Queen Elizabeth's time.

We wandered through the narrow ancient streets, and climbed up on to the wall to look over the compact little town. We got the key of the great church from the caretaker who lives nearby, and went inside that enormous, beautiful, and very historic building. It seems hardly used as a church any more; there were cobwebs and dead leaves everywhere. It was built in the thirteenth century on the site of a church built by the Danes in the eleventh century, and one of the Earls of Desmond added a chancel and the magnificent decorated east window in 1498. It is a building crammed with historical monuments, more of a museum than a place of worship, now owned by the Church of Ireland and with a minute congregation.

119

But Youghal is full of ancient and historical buildings. Ones I noticed were the Protestant Asylum, dated 1838; an almshouse for decayed soldiers (I was tempted to bang on the door to see if they would take me in since I answer to that description); Tynte's Castle, originally built on the shore though the sea has since receded here; and some fine warehouses along the present shore, one of them now a modern carpet factory. There are three semi-enclosed docks, full of fishing boats; there are many fine pubs; and, if you like eating fish and if money is absolutely no object to you, there is always Ahernes fish restaurant. Youghal would be a fine little town to live in — if you like small old towns and the sea that is — a great place to keep a small boat. Sir Walter Raleigh, however, grew tired of his Irish estate once he had destroyed all the oak forest on it. He sold it to Richard Boyle, afterwards Earl of Cork, and went back to live in England. He was ill-advised to do so for, in 1618, he had his head cut off.

We drove up the beautiful Blackwater, spectacular between wooded banks, with the odd ruined Fitzgerald castle half-hidden in the trees. The country here has a very feudal feel to it. It seems to be a land where the great estates still exist. The various Irish rebellions do not seem to have had much effect here. We left the car and walked across fields and over rough country towards the river. We came upon an old deserted yeoman's farmhouse — good farm buildings, a substantial farmhouse, a yard, or haggard — all overgrown with nettles and brambles. The place was semi-ruined, but we found books lying about inside, including a boy's school exercise book, dated from the 1930s. We leafed through it, feeling that we were getting an intimate glimpse into the past, and wondering where the owner of the book is now, whether he is alive or dead, and whether he is still in Ireland or has emigrated to some far country. He was a bright boy, and I would give him ten out of ten for spelling.

At Cappoquin, which is as far up as the tide goes and where the Blackwater makes a right-angle turn to the westward (if you are going up it), we seemed confirmed in our idea of this being a feudal place. An enormous man, with an exceedingly loud voice and exaggerated upper-class English accent, had just come ashore from water-skiing. He had one hench-man to drive the speedboat that towed him and another to drive the Rolls Royce that waited to take him away. I was quite sure that he was a naval or military man, but will never know his rank for he was wearing nothing but a very small pair of bathing trunks. The size of his belly, which overhung this garment, indicated that he had been at least an admiral. His great voice reverberated about the valley as though he was trying to make himself heard above the din of battle.

We proceeded up that lovely river, non-tidal now, to Lismore. Here a castle of overpowering magnificence dominates the river. We crossed the bridge to reach it, and wandered round the little town which, although not much more than a village, is presumably a city because it has two cathedrals. The little place seems to be completely dominated by, and in awe of the castle; it has a subdued atmosphere. The castle was originally built by Prince John before that unpopular man became king of England in 1185 on the desecrated site of one of the holiest places in Ireland, the shrine and college of Saint Carthagh, or Carthage. The college he founded in the seventh century became famous throughout Europe, and it is said that King Alfred of England studied there.

After the site had been desecrated and destroyed in order to build the castle, the Irish, outraged, attacked and sacked the castle. Pilgrims began to return and it became a sacred place again. King John decided to compromise and ruled that it could become the centre of a bishopric again provided that no native (i.e. Irish) cleric should ever be the bishop. No native Irish family has ever made the castle its residence and at present it belongs to the sister of the late Fred Astaire. She married into the Devonshire family, which had come into possession of the castle and whole huge estate in 1748 by marriage. She visits the castle occasionally with her present husband for a short holiday. I hope she sometimes gives a thought to Saint Carthagh but I suppose she lives in a very different world from that ascetic saint. The saint's holy well remains, sited in the private grounds of the castle, but there is a spout in the wall of the castle grounds from which its water dribbles, which is intended for the benefit of any pilgrim who wishes to bless himself with it. Every year, on the Pattern Day (14 May), the castle is opened and the well made fully accessible to the hoi polloi.

Apart from being the burial place of a holy saint, Lismore has another, quite different sort of man altogether, interred in it: one Myler McGrath. He was consecrated bishop of Down and Connor by the Pope in 1567, but only two years later discovered that his conscience obliged him to change his allegiance from the Holy Father to Queen Elizabeth, the new head of the Anglican Church, and so he became an apostate. Could the fact that the old faith had been proscribed by the English government have had anything to do with this rapid conversion? After all, the Archbishop of Cashel had his head cut off on the orders of Queen Elizabeth because

121

he refused to recognize her as Head of the Christian Church at about this time.

McGrath took over as the new Archbishop of Cashel at about this time, and was also made bishop of Lismore and Waterford. From this position of power, he amassed no less than 77 benefices, from every one of which he drew an income. And lest he should feel the pinch of penury, he granted the bishop's palace and all the lands that went with it to Sir Walter Raleigh, in perpetuity, for thirteen pounds six and eightpence a year. One can imagine Saint Carthagh's spirit, if it keeps an eye on its old home, looking down at these developments with some disapproval.

Anyway, Sir Walter Raleigh sold the whole damn lot — the castle, bishop's palace, town and vast estate – to a man named Richard Boyle for £1,500. Thrown in with this were the towns of Youghal, Cappoquin and of course Lismore itself. Boyle was one of the first of the really successful self-made millionaires. He arrived on the shores of Dublin on 23 June 1588, and, in his own words:

'When I arrived in Dublin all my wealth was £27 3s in money and two tokens that my mother had given me viz a diamond ring — which I ever have since and still wear and a bracelet of gold worth £10, a taffety doublet cut with and upon taffety — a pair of black velvet breeches, laced, a new milan fustion suit laced and cut upon taffety, two cloaks, competent linen and necessaries, with my rapier and dagger.'

He managed to add to his small stock of possessions by marrying the right lady, an heiress from Limerick, who died almost immediately, leaving him £500 a year. He invested his money very successfully by buying, for practically nothing, the confiscated estates of the Irish nobility. Soon he had a vast estate and a vast fortune. He did so well that his neighbours became jealous, and accused him of conniving with the King of Spain. He had to go to London, twice, to clear his name, which he did successfully, and became a favourite of Queen Elizabeth. Of course that monarch's preoccupation with Ireland and determination to subjugate it were caused by her fear of Spain. And if the Spanish Armada, instead of making up-Channel for the Lowlands Low, had sailed into Waterford Harbour, fought the English in Ireland, and raised and armed the Irish, there is no doubt that Spain would have conquered England: the whole history of the world would have been very different.

So Richard Boyle rose from, well, a taffety doublet to riches, and married another rich woman, the daughter of Sir John Fenton, Master of the Rolls. Together they had fourteen children: seven girls and seven boys. Four of the boys became lords and most of the girls were married into the nobility. One of the sons was Robert Boyle, who invented 'Boyle's Law', with which I had to wrestle at school, and is called the father of modern chemistry.

Among numerous other titles, Richard was created Earl of Cork. Before he died he built no less than two enormous and very ugly monuments to himself: one in Saint Patrick's Cathedral in Dublin and one in the cathedral at Lismore, since he wasn't quite sure in which place he would eventually peg out. In the event, it was in Lismore, and he is buried there in the old Catholic cathedral, now, of course, the Protestant one. (The Catholics had to build a new one for themselves because the old one was taken away from them.)

The subsequent history of Lismore Castle is less eventful, but in 1811 the Duke of Devonshire of the time (known as 'the bachelor Duke') substantially enlarged the castle with stone quarried and cut in Derbyshire.

On the way back from Lismore, returning to our stately caravan near Youghal, we came to the valley of the River Bride on the outskirts of the small town of Tallow. 'Must be a farm sale on,' I said to Angela, for we found cars parked alongside the country road. But soon we were brought to a halt by a great throng of cars, horseboxes, trailers, horses and people. We got out and pushed through the crowd, and walked, or rather shoved and threaded our way, for about a mile. There were thousands of people and hundreds of horses, donkeys even. There were farmers, rich ones and not-so-rich ones, and some a bit rough; and Tinkers, or Itinerants as they should be called; and horse-faced ladies in tweeds. Sellers were trying to trot their nags along the crowded road through the mass of people, and noisy bargaining was going on all around, with excited onlookers urging on the actual protagonists to make a deal: 'Come on, give the man what he's askin' for! She's a lovely filly.' And we actually saw a horse sold for £11,000, with all the consequent clapping of the right hands of buyer and seller and even the writing out of a cheque there and then.

We tried to get into a pub, for the crowd had made us thirsty, but without any success. To get within several yards of the bar was impossible, and the din in the bar-room was deafening. But we managed, eventually, to get our car through the mêlée, and out the other side, and came to a lonely pub called the Halfway House. There were just a few Landrovers and

123

horseboxes outside, and when we went in we could get to the bar quite easily. I had a long conversation with a horsey-looking gentleman who was drinking cider, a lot of it. I don't know whether he could make head or tail of my own English accent, but for a long time I thought he was addressing me in Irish. We were having a most interesting conversation — certainly a more enlightening one than one generally gets — without either of us being able to understand a word of what the other was saying.

Finally I turned to Angela and said, 'Angela, the man talks Irish.'

She burst out laughing. 'He doesn't know a word of it,' she said. 'It's gibberish; it's the cider in him talking; he's just talking gibberish.'

I listened carefully after that, and realized that she was correct. Occasionally there were a few words of comprehensible West Waterford English, but the rest was a jumble of gibberish that might have meant anything.

Cider is not a normal drink in Ireland, although some apples are grown near Clonmel in the Suir Valley and there is a factory there, and you can only get it in selected pubs. But the Irish, generally, have great respect for the substance, and credit it with much greater powers than it really has. Take as witness the following, very popular song, called 'Johnny Jump Up':

> *I'll tell you a story that happened to me*
> *One day as I went down to Youghal by the sea.*
> *The sun it was bright and the day it was warm,*
> *Says I, 'A quiet pint wouldn't do me no harm.'*
>
> *I went in and I called for a bottle of stout.*
> *Says the bar man, 'I'm sorry all the beer is sold out.*
> *Try whiskey or Paddy, ten years in the wood.'*
> *Says I, 'I'll try cider, I hear that it's good.'*
>
> *Chorus:*
> *Oh never, oh never, oh never again,*
> *If I live to a hundred or a hundred and ten*
> *For I fell to the ground and I couldn't get up*
> *After drinking a quart of the Johnny Jump Up.*
>
> *After leaving the third I went to the yard*
> *Where I bumped into Brophy, the big civic guard*

'Come here to me boy, don't you know I'm the law?'
I upped with me fist and I shattered his jaw.

He fell to the ground with his knees doubled up,
But it wasn't I hit him, 'twas Johnny Jump Up.
The next thing I met down in Youghal by the sea
Was a cripple on crutches and says he to me,

'I'm afraid of me life I'll be hit by a car.
Won't you help me across to the Railway Men's bar?'
After drinking a quart of that cider so sweet
He threw down his crutches and danced in the street.

I went up the Lee road a friend for to see,
And they call it the mad house in Cork by the Lee,
But when I got up there, the truth I do tell,
They had the poor bugger locked up in a cell.

Chorus:

> *Oh never, oh never, oh never again,*
> *If I live to a hundred or a hundred and ten*
> *For I fell to the ground and I couldn't get up*
> *After drinking a quart of the Johnny Jump Up.*

Said the guard, testing him, 'Say these words if you can:
Around the rugged rock the ragged rascal ran.'
'Tell them I'm not crazy, tell them I'm not mad,
It was only a sup of the bottle I had.'

Chorus:

> *Oh never, oh never, oh never again,*
> *If I live to a hundred or a hundred and ten*
> *For I fell to the ground and I couldn't get up*
> *After drinking a quart of the Johnny Jump Up.*

A man died in the Union by the name of McNabb.
They washed him and laid him outside on a slab,
And after O'Connor his measurements did take,
His wife took him home to a bloody fine wake.

About twelve o'clock and the beer it was high
When the corpse he sat up and says he with a sigh,
'I can't get to heaven, they won't let me up,
Till I bring them a quart of the Johnny Jump Up.'

Chorus:
    Oh never, oh never, oh never again,
    If I live to a hundred or a hundred and ten
    For I fell to the ground and I couldn't get up
    After drinking a quart of the Johnny Jump Up.

CHAPTER FOURTEEN

~

Cork and Its Patron Saint

BEAUTIFUL, FRUITFUL, FERTILE COUNTRYSIDE all the way to Cork — it's no wonder that the Elizabethan adventurers found the place so attractive for settlement. As we rolled along the main road we came to a sign that pointed to the left and said: Cathedral. Wondering why a cathedral should be sited so far from any town or city, we followed the sign, and drove over some wooded hills, back down on to the plain again, and into the tiny village of Cloyne.

Tiny the village might have been — in fact it hardly even qualified as a hamlet — but just outside of it stood a huge ecclesiastical building, obviously the cathedral, and not far away stood the ruined base of a round tower. The huge cathedral looked most incongruous in that depopulated landscape; the entire population of the adjacent hamlet would not have filled one pew.

Saint Colman founded a monastery here in the eighth century, when England was still plunged deep in the pagan Dark Ages, and the building that we now see was probably built in the thirteenth century. There is a beautiful alabaster effigy of Bishop Berkeley inside, made by a Bruce Joy. Berkeley was bishop of Cloyne from 1734 to 1753. He is said to have been generous to the starving people around him, and was something of a philosopher. He supported the theory that matter does not really exist, but that what we perceive to be matter is only images we have in our minds. When Dr Johnson, that sturdy realist, was asked what he thought about this theory, that matter does not exist, he maintained that it does exist. When pressed to prove it, he kicked a stone and said, 'I prove it thus.' No-one has ever come up with a satisfactory counter-argument. But, whatever we thought of his philosophies, it was bizarre to come so completely unexpectedly upon the great Bishop Berkeley's tomb in such a remote and unpeopled place. We do not read guide books, so if we find

127

such things as this they always come as a surprise, which is as it should be, I think.

We decided to have a look at Cobh, which was and still is the main port of Cork Harbour, allowing ships to sail up the Lee to the very centre of Cork city itself. Cobh (pronounced cove) is the terminus for ferries to Wales, cruise ships, and was for a long time an important naval base. We once saw a Russian warship lying there, while its well-dressed and very well-behaved Russian matelots wandered through the city in large groups.

Cobh is on an island, connected to the rest of the world by a causeway. To get to it by car you have to cross Foaty Island, on which we discovered the enormous and sumptuous mansion called Fota House. Decorated inside with an elaborate sumptuousness, the place is full of paintings, many by Irish artists. The whole place was built and decorated with magnificent taste, and on a most lavish scale. The park, which fills the entire island, is 780 acres.

The man who took the quid or two it cost us to enter told us that this place had been bought from the previous owners in 1975 by Cork University College, and that the Royal Zoological Society had opened the Wildlife Park, which we did not have time to see, a little later. Now, however, the place has been bought by some British entertainment industry company.

We later dug out the history of the place, as much as we wanted to know. Originally it had been a hunting box owned by the Smith-Barry family, enlarged as a permanent mansion in the 1820s. In 1847, at the height of the great Irish famine, one of the family records that he: 'crossed in the boat from Bristol to Cork; my father met us with a six-oared gig at Passage, and we landed at the Tower where a carriage met us, and we were dragged by the labourers up to the house.' When the Hon. Mrs Bell and her husband Major Bertram came to take over the house in 1915 their carriage too was dragged to the house by the servants. There is a photograph taken in 1940 of the Bells surrounded by no less than forty servants, nearly all male, which indicates that there was probably an equal number of maids tucked away somewhere else. The family owned 27,000 acres in all, besides Foaty Island, so no doubt they managed to extract enough rent from the wretched tenants to pay 'em all.

I find something very perverse about such houses. It is almost obscene that at a time when people were starving to death, and when even those not starving were having to exist in leaking, falling-down hovels, all that money and effort went into contriving this palace of luxury for one family.

What had they done to deserve it? It may be argued that at least the forty servants employed by the house were not starving: they, at least, were saved from the famine and from the direst poverty. Yes, but there would have been no famine, there would have been no poverty if it were not for the rack-renting needed to finance the running of the house. In 1841, a few years before the famine, when all the magnificence of Fota House — with its arboretum, water gardens, tropical gardens, and all the rest of it, like a hundred other such mansions in Ireland — was still being built, the English novelist and nobility-lover Thackeray was travelling through Ireland. This is what he had to say on reaching Cork:

'And so it is through the south and west of Ireland; the traveller is haunted by the face of the popular starvation. It is not the exception, it is the condition of the people. In this fairest and richest of countries, men are suffering and starving by millions. There are thousands of them at this minute stretched in the sunshine at their cabin doors with no work, scarcely any food, no hope seemingly. Strong countrymen are lying in bed *'for the hunger'* — because a man lying on his back does not need so much food as a person afoot. Many of them have torn up the unripe potatoes from their little gardens to exist now, and must look to winter, when they shall have to suffer starvation and cold too. The epicurean, and the traveller for pleasure, had better travel anywhere than here; where there are miseries one does not dare to think of; where one is always feeling how helpless pity is, and how hopeless relief, and is perpetually ashamed of being happy.'

The Irish poor were forced to subsist on potatoes since it was the one crop that the agents of the landlords could not easily seize. Barley, oats or wheat had to be harvested and stored at the proper time so it was easy to find an opportunity to take them. Potatoes, however, could be, and were, left in the ground and dug up right through the winter as required. No landlord or his agent was going to go to the trouble of digging them up.

Therefore, when I look at places like Fota House I do not rejoice that they were built for they were founded on injustice. But I do rejoice that they are now open for us all to see and use. Good uses could be found for every one of them, uses that would benefit the descendants of the people who actually dressed and laid the stone from which they are built, and who gave up three-quarters of their crops in rent to the idle landlords for whom they were built.

129

Thackeray did not understand the causes of rural Irish poverty, but he was a humane man, and hated to see hunger and misery. He has this to say about a place he found in Kildare:

'Stretching away from the Kilcullen Bridge, for a couple of miles or more ... is to be seen a much prettier sight, I think, than the finest park and mansion in the world. This is a tract of excessively green land, dotted over with brilliant white cottages, each with its couple of trim acres of garden, where you see thick potato ridges covered with blossom, great blue patches of comfortable cabbages, and such pleasant plants of the poor man's garden. Two or three years since, the land was a marshy common, which had never since the days of the Deluge fed any being bigger than a snipe, and into which the poor people descended, draining and cultivating, and rescuing the marsh from the water, and raising their cabins and setting up their little enclosures of two or three acres upon the land which they had thus created. "Many of 'em has passed months in jail for that," said my informant (a groom on the back seat of my host's phaeton); for it appears that certain gentlemen in the neighbourhood looked upon the titles of these new colonists with some jealousy ...'

But better council prevailed as there was at least one humane landlord in that district, 'and there are now two hundred flourishing little homesteads upon this rescued land, and as many families in comfort and plenty.' When I read this last sentence in Thackeray's book I wanted to wave the book about and give a mighty cheer, for it warmed my heart. If you give a family its fair share of the earth's surface and leave it in peace, the members of that family will soon find a way of living 'in comfort and plenty' if they are any good at all.

Well, having seen Fota House, and having thought all these thoughts, we continued southwards until we came to the bridge across to Great Island, on which stands Cobh. Across the bridge is a Martello tower and an ancient castle. There are so many ancient castles in Ireland that, in the end, one is apt not to bother to look at them.

Cobh, when we got to it, reeks of the sea: sailing ships (although there are none there now of course), Nelson, and sailors in short blue jackets and pig-tails. The town is crammed in between a steep hillside and the sea; the houses are jumbled together, one row of them looking down on the roofs of the row below, and the streets are narrow. The whole place is dominated

130

now by an enormous cathedral. It is built on an eminence, so that it towers over the town and is no doubt seen from far and wide across the ocean.

This mighty edifice was, like all the Catholic churches and cathedrals in Ireland, built with the pennies of the poor. The Church of England of course had taken over the original cathedral of this diocese: the cathedral we had seen near the tiny hamlet of Cloynes. So the Catholics decided, when they were allowed to have cathedrals again, that they had to have a new cathedral. They built it here at Cobh, and dedicated it to Saint Colman, who was the founder of Cloynes. For the people of Cobh it came to take the place of the Mass Cave at East Ferry. This had been used right through the penal times for celebrating Mass: the cave served as the sanctuary and the congregation sat on the ground outside. In 1657, a Major Morgan, Member of Parliament for Wicklow, was able to say in parliament, to general agreement and acclaim: 'We have two beasts in Ireland that lay burdens on us. The first, the wolf, for whom we pay £5 a head if a dog, and £10 if a bitch. The second a priest, on whose head we lay £10, if eminent more.' And so they hid in caves. But in 1868 the penal laws against Catholics were abolished, so the people could move from the cave to the cathedral. In fact by the reign of George I, 'chapels', or 'mass houses' were allowed to exist quite openly — provided they were not called 'churches' — and priests were free to practise — provided they were licensed. No bishops of course.

If you love the sea, and ships, and small crowded seaports, Cobh would be the place for you. From it you look out over the wide waters of Cork Harbour, where ships still come and go. The Royal Cork Yacht Club has its clubhouse here, and it is said to be the first yacht club in existence. Cobh was the point of departure for America for hundreds of thousands of starving emigrants during the hungry 1800s; and Spike Island, which you can see out in the bay, was the place of imprisonment for thousands more awaiting transportation to the penal colony in Australia. There is a memorial near the waterfront to the people who died in the *Lusitania* when she was sunk by a German submarine in the First World War. Hundreds of dead lie buried in the old graveyard near Cobh.

We drove back to the mainland and on, to Cork itself, and parked our little home on wheels in a camping site near Cork airport. Here all the signs are in French as well as English, because of the numbers of French people who land at the airport, or at Ringaskiddy from ferry ships, and stay here a night or two before faring further to the west.

Cork city is a beautiful and ancient place. Much of it is built on an island made by the bifurcation of the River Lee. Some of the main streets were water once but foolish city councils filled them in and made streets of them. You can tell that they were water because the old Georgian houses that line them show, by their entrances, that they once lined a navigable waterway. (You will see the same arrangement in Amsterdam, where the inhabitants have had the sense to retain their canals and not fill them in.) The arrangement is: an ordinary front door which opens on to the street that ran alongside the canal, and then, a storey lower, a water door which opened directly on to the canal so that goods could be unloaded from ships straight into the basement of the building through a tunnel under the road. There are, too, in Cork, buildings with very Dutch-looking gables, showing that there must have been quite a Netherlandish influence in days of yore. There was no doubt a lot of trade with the Low Countries.

Cork, I imagine, would be a fine city to live in. There is a plethora of fine pubs. Some of these are well described in that naughty book by Honor Tracy, *Mind You, I've Said Nothing!* There is an hilarious description of a search for a somewhat bibulous professor through various purlieus of the town. The search for the professor reminds me very much of a search I made myself, in Dublin, for an old friend of mine named Seamus Innes. Seamus was an Irish piper and collector of folk songs and music, and he used to come and stay with me when I lived in Suffolk. We used to sally out together trying to get old men to sing folk songs. Seamus would lean up against this or that bar counter ('a long, sad streak of Celtic twilight' I once heard somebody call him) and, after a pint or two, out of his pocket would come a tin whistle. He would play it so brilliantly that the local worthies present would drag old Suffolk folk songs out of their subconscious, and I would have to go to the car to get the tape recorder to capture the event for posterity.

Well, on that long-ago visit to Dublin (decades before I ever thought of living there), I went to the RTE building (the Irish equivalent of the BBC) to enquire for Seamus. Immediately I mentioned his name a knot of people began to surround me: the doorman, the security man, various passing producers, members of the public, secretaries, and, for all I know, the Director General himself.

A most lively discussion followed. Would he be, by this hour, in Maloney's, or in Sweeney's, or in ... and a dozen other names of hostelries followed. Eventually some sort of consensus was arrived at, as the cluster of my advisers got bigger and bigger, and I was sent off, with many expressions of good will and wishes for my success, to the pub considered the most likely.

'You've just this minute missed him,' said the landlord. I had to have a pint of course. 'He'll be below at Murphy's,' said one customer. 'Never!' said another. 'I heard him talk of Callaghan's.'

I swallowed my pint, tried Callaghan's, drew a blank, tried Murphy's. 'He was in here an hour ago. He'll be above at Clary's.'

I followed him most of the day, but it was like chasing a will-o'-the-wisp: he ever faded before me. And there was the dreaded deadline of Holy Hour to meet. During Holy Hour, which lasts for two hours in the afternoon, you can neither get into, nor get out of, a Dublin pub. If you are out you are out, if you are in you are in. I just managed by the skin of my teeth to get in, to find no Seamus and in I had to stay for the space of many, many pints. After we were all let out I was in no mood to hunt further. I had to catch the boat that day, and so never met my good, old friend; and never saw him again, for he moved to the land of fine musicians up in the sky. A fine musician he was too, and a man whose company I loved. Honor Tracy found her professor, though, after a similar chase, and the description of the hunt is well worth the reading.

But Cork is not only a city of pubs: it is a city of culture of other sorts too. We went to the art gallery and saw many fine paintings in it, a magnificent Epstein, and some most impressive stained-glass work by Harry Clarke. We went to the Opera House and saw a brilliant play called *Big Maggie*, by J. B. Keane. (Keane is fairly old now but there is a handful of most excellent young playwrights in Ireland today.) There is a fine university in Cork, too. I have been asked to give talks there and have been delighted by the intelligence and liveliness of the audience. Cork is just the right size for a city and I wish we lived closer to it for, if we did, I would go there far more often. Dublin has grown too big. When cities become excessively swollen, the things that one values most about them do not grow: only the population grows, and the sprawling, soulless suburbs, and the residential estates. The true culture, in fact, seems to shrink.

Cork was founded, like nearly every place in Ireland, by a saint. Saint Finbarr (or Barry), who died in AD 633 at Cloyne, was actually buried in the monastery that he had founded at Cork. On his grave and shrine the Church of Ireland built a huge cathedral, completing it in 1870 (was it an Anglican answer to that huge RC job in Cobh, I wonder?). But Saint Finbarr's most famous residence, and the place where he spent most of his life, was far up the River Lee — at its very source in fact — on the lake-island of Gougane Barra.

On 30 September there was to be a pilgrimage to this place, so we felt compelled to go there. How anybody who was living in that magical place could have left it I do not know, but the saint apparently had a dream which told him to travel down the river Lee and found a monastery near its mouth. Thus was founded Cork (in Irish, *Corcaigh*, a marsh).

You drive through rocky, hilly, broken and well-wooded country along a narrow lane, and eventually come to this magical lake surrounded by high wooded hills. And in the middle of the lake is a little island. We got there in the morning, when few people were there. A causeway gives foot access to the island, and over it we went, to find a modern chapel and some older monastic cells set around a sunken courtyard with a great cross in it. The cells were restored by a nineteenth-century monk, who lived in them. There are large holly trees on the island and the little place has a feeling of great sanctity. If you cannot feel holiness there you will feel it nowhere. There is a large hotel nearby on the mainland, and I couldn't help feeling what a fine place it was for a holiday, particularly if you liked holy places, or fishing for trout.

Gradually people began to arrive, some on foot as pilgrims should, but most like us: in horseless carriages. A great throng gathered; there were hundreds of adults and hundreds of children. They drifted on to the island until it was covered with them. Then priests arrived, and, standing in front of the Romanesque chapel, celebrated the Mass. There was dead silence from that multitude, even from the children, as Mass was said, and then we all partook of the consecrated bread. The weather was magnificent, and it was a most moving and beautiful occasion. I shall remember it as long as I live.

CHAPTER FIFTEEN

~

The Tailor of Kerry

OUR NEXT DESTINATION WAS KINSALE, to see if my old friend Hedley McNeice was still alive. She, her husband Louis, and their little daughter used to come to my home in Suffolk, and Louis would stretch himself out on my lawn in the sun looking like *le poète élongé*. After Louis died, Hedley had moved to Kinsale and opened a restaurant there. So we left the caravan site near Cork airport, and, after following and then crossing a beautiful estuary, and then another, we arrived at a little town of such beauty that it was almost too much to take in. We went into a pub and enquired after Hedley.

'Hedley?' said the barman. 'She moved to France. And I hear she's dead, God rest her.' But he had fond memories of her, as did everyone else we met in that town. 'When I last saw her', he said, 'she met me at her door wearing a weird dressing gown and holding a gigantic fish under her arm. She was a great lady. Everyone loved her.'

We sought out another old friend, the silversmith Pat Dolan. He used to live near New Ross and we used to drink together in Richie Roche's Bar. He now has a workshop on a prime site in Kinsale.

'I should have come here years ago,' he said. 'Property's terribly expensive but you do make a living here.'

The place is now entirely, or almost entirely, given over to the tourist industry. It is an ancient and very beautiful town, made more so (over the top, some people might think) by a tremendous self-consciousness on the part of the burghers. Every house is beautifully painted and looked after; the shop fronts are all in perfect taste; there are scores of up-market craft shops, and restaurants galore (indeed, for anybody wishing to dig their grave with their teeth, Kinsale would be a splendid place to do it in). Most of the shops seem to be run by Irish but patronized by foreigners.

135

This little town played an enormous part in the sad and bloody history of Ireland. Angela and I stood on the battlements of James Fort, one of the two fortifications that commanded the harbour, and tried to imagine the many stormings and siegings the town had been subjected to.

After the Desmond rebellion, when the Fitzgerald family and such of the Irish aristocracy as were left were so defeated by Queen Elizabeth's forces that the survivors, in Spenser's words: 'looked like anatomies of death, they spake like ghosts crying out from their graves,' things must have seemed desperate for the Irish in the south of Ireland. In the north, though, The O'Neill, and The O'Donnell (whose descendants it had been my fortune to meet in Austria on the great Salzburg Raid) and other Irish chieftains were still managing to hold out against the English and the Scots. The Spanish Armada had tried to attack England but had failed because the English had by then gained control of the sea. Two years later, in October 1601, the Spanish got together another armada and had another go. They did what they should have done in the first place: they sent a fleet and a small army to Ireland. But it was too little and too late. They made their customary balls-up of it. They meant to land in northern Ireland and join forces with the Irish rebels there, but they landed at Kinsale instead, which forced the Irish forces in Ulster to march south, in the middle of a very bad winter. By the time they got to Kinsale the town was already invested by an English army and the Irish were exhausted. O'Neill wanted to wait before attacking but the Spanish commander, Don Juan Aquila, persuaded him to get on with battle. The Irish army was completely defeated and such was the slaughter that it is said that the Bandon river ran red with their blood.

The Spanish promptly asked for terms, and were allowed to sail away back to Spain intact. But with this battle Irish resistance was completely broken, and what had been left of the old Celtic way of life in Ireland utterly extinguished. The O'Donnell fled to Spain and, as I described, I met his descendant in Austria — an Austrian count with no trace of the Irish about him. O'Neill got back to Ulster and then surrendered to the English, losing his power and lands as a result. Ireland was henceforth completely an English colony, and most of the old Irish nobility left. If the southern Irish chieftains had joined forces with O'Neill the story would have been different. Some did, and of course lost their lands by doing so. The O'Driscolls and the O'Sullivans were among these. But the O'Briens, the Burkes and the McCarthys felt that discretion was the better part of valour. Six years after the events at Kinsale came 'The Flight of the Earls':

the Ulster chieftains, with their retainers, took ship to France, never to return.

The English, realizing the importance of Kinsale, proceeded to fortify it heavily. Henceforth no Irish were allowed inside its gates. But in 1641, when the Civil War had broken out in England, some of the landowners in Munster rose in rebellion against King Charles I. It was the worst thing they could have done. An English army, together with the citizens of Kinsale who were loyal to the king, quickly destroyed them. One castle near Kinsale, Carriganas, the lord of which had come out in rebellion, was set on fire by the Kinsale men. Their leader, Tristran Whetcombe, the Sovereign (Mayor) of Kinsale, described the event thus: 'The fire continued all night and the next day until at last, were brought forth such a pack of roasted rogues as never in man's lifetime were seen and at last, as many as were not roasted enough were hanged.' In those days it did not pay to be on the wrong side.

But the town's loyalty to the King did not help it, for very soon Cromwell arrived. He bombarded the town, took over the keys and installed his military governor. Tristran Whetcombe had backed the wrong side.

But Kinsale's troubles were not over. James II arrived from France, to where he had fled after William of Orange had kicked him out of England, and landed at Kinsale. He was greeted with rapture by the Catholic Irish, but if they had known how much good he was going to do them they would have chucked him straight back into the sea. After he had fled from the Battle of the Boyne (long before the battle was over) he managed to get to Duncannon, near my house, from where he took ship to Kinsale. There, a French ship was waiting and he was taken back to France. The Williamite forces besieged and stormed Kinsale and took it. Such of the defenders as got away went to Limerick, where the Irish still held out, and, after the famous treaty with William's forces, joined the second great 'Flight of the Wild Geese'. And so they left for the Continent to take service under various foreign kings.

In spite of such hardships, Kinsale shows every sign now of having been an extremely prosperous small seaport, right up until ships got too big to get into the harbour. It was, too, a great centre of fisheries. English, Scottish and even French fishing boats used to gather there for the herring and mackerel. The fish were landed and salted in barrels and sent all over northern Europe. There was a strong local fishing fleet too, and there were the Kinsale Hookers, the south coast equivalent of the better-known Galway ones. Plenty of Galway Hookers are left, not one Kinsale one alas. The huge shoals of herring, pilchards and mackerel are also no more, but there is still a fishing fleet and a lot of yachts, so the atmosphere of a real seaport town still lingers in Kinsale to give it its great charm and interest.

Well, not being in the right income bracket to eat in any of Kinsale's excellent restaurants, we headed west again. We reached the Atlantic at Bantry Bay, and continued round the shore to Glengarriff. Bantry Bay was the venue for one of the many incompetent attempts of the enemies of England to use Ireland as a jumping-off place. In 1796, in the middle of the winter gales, a force of 15,000 well-armed French troops led by General Hoche sailed from Brest. All their forty-three ships evaded the English blockade, but half of them then got lost, and the other half, although they dropped anchor in Bantry Bay, did not actually land because the bold general felt it imprudent. The Irish patriot Wolfe Tone was aboard one of the ships, and he reported later that 'he could have tossed a biscuit on to the shore.' The United Irishmen were, at that time, ripe to stage their rebellion, and with a force like that (of well-armed professional soldiers), they certainly would have prevailed in the '98 rebellion instead of being defeated. But no, the French sailed back to France again and nothing came of it at all.

If the French had taken the trouble to come ashore, they would have seen how beautiful the place is. I must quote my old friend Thackeray again:

'The harbour is beautiful. Small mountains in green undulations rising on the opposite side; great grey ones further back; a pretty island in the midst of the water, which is wonderfully bright and calm. A handsome yacht, and two or three vessels with their Sunday colours out were lying in the bay. It looked like a seaport scene at a theatre, gay, cheerful, neat and picturesque. At a little distance the town, too, is very pretty. There are some smart houses on the quays, a handsome court-house as usual, a fine large hotel, and plenty of people flocking round the wonderful coach.'

But, as was usual for him in Ireland, the beauty of the countryside was marred by the poverty of its inhabitants:

'With the exception of this street and the quay, with their whitewashed and slated houses, it is a town of cabins. The wretchedness of some of them is quite curious . . . I tried to make a sketch of a row which lean against an old wall . . . it was vain to try; one might as well make a sketch of a bundle of rags. An ordinary pigsty in England is really more comfortable. Most of them were not six feet long and five feet high, built of stones huddled together, a hole being left for the people to creep in at, a ruined thatch to keep out some little portion of the rain. The occupiers of these places sat at their doors in tolerable contentment, or the children came down and washed their feet in the water. I declare I believe a Hottentot kraal has more comforts in it: even to write of the place makes one unhappy, and the words move slow.'

To this state had greedy landlords reduced a proud people, in one of the most fertile countries in the world. You can search where you will in the Republic of Ireland today to find dwellings such as Thackeray described and you will not find them, thank God.

As for Glengarriff, beyond Bantry Bay, it is all too picturesque for words. Angela could only gasp with astonishment at the beauty of it. Even Thackeray was 'beat' as the Irish say. He had to enlist an imaginary army of Victorian landscape painters to do the place justice: 'I would like to be a great prince, and bring a train of painters over to make, if they could, and according to their several capabilities, a set of pictures of the place.' The village (which reminds one somewhat of a Swiss ski resort because it is almost all hotels and pensions) is set between the bay and some steep incredibly rocky and craggy hills, with high mountains beyond. The huge boulders that litter the narrow littoral are hidden and clothed by a luxuriance of near-tropical vegetation, for the extremely rainy climate, the Gulf Stream, and the protection from the north winds of the mountains, make for a lushness which is untypical of northern Europe.

We had to tear ourselves away from this beautiful place because I wanted to visit my old friend the Tailor of Kerry. When I stated at the beginning of this book that I had not been to Ireland until after I saw those mystical mountains over the Irish Sea I was, well, perhaps not being a liar, but at least a stranger to the truth. Or can I claim poetic licence?

I *had* been to Ireland, but it was so long ago, so remote, it seems as if it was in a different life. It was certainly in a different age. I lived in a sailing boat at that time, generally moored somewhere on the east coast of England. I suddenly got an urge, and took a train to Fishguard. I arrived there in the middle of the night and thought what a mysterious place it seemed, stuck out there in the far west of Wales. Looking out of the train window into the dark night, and seeing strange fields and woods and trees and the glint of the stars on a river, I thought it looked a mysterious land. I little thought that for seventeen years it would be my home.

Once over the sea in Ireland I took a train to Kenmare. Why Kenmare? Because I had some vague idea that the west coast of Ireland was the place to go (like every other tourist before and since), and Kenmare was on the railway. I hired a bicycle and cycled along the south shore of Kenmare Bay, until I came to a scattering of little houses around an inlet behind the bay and a pub called Teddy O'Sullivan's Bar. I went in, quenched a well-earned thirst, and somebody rented me a cottage, or cabin, for a shilling or two a week.

I was writing a book at the time, about Africa as it happened, a continent in which I had spent much of my life. It was March, very cold and windy, and it seldom stopped raining. Every day I found time to go for a walk. If it was simply teeming with rain, any person I met would say, in a soft Irish voice, ''Tis a soft day.' For a few days I could go to the pub and get wet inside as well as out; but one day the door of that establishment was closed, and nothing I could do would get it opened again.

It took about a week for me to find out the reason for this: it was Lent; and the pubs in that area simply did not open during Lent. I was surprised, though, at how few people I saw about the village and the lanes. But one day, after I had been for a wet walk, I happened to be passing the pub and all was revealed to me. The door opened a chink and O'Sullivan himself peered out. 'Go round to the back,' he hissed. I did so, the back door was opened and in I went, to find the whole male population of the town in there. After that, as they say, I never looked back as far as having a well-earned drink was concerned.

As for my other needs most of them were provided for without any effort or expense on my part at all. I wanted milk? A pretty little girl delivered a bottle of it to my door every day. Could I pay her? I could not. 'Sure we'd be milkin' anyway. There's no cost to it.' There were three small fishing trawlers in the place, which caught quantities of *nethrops*, or Dublin Bay prawns. They had no buyers for these and usually threw them back. When they heard I liked them they always brought back a bag for me. Again, they would not let me pay for them. No vegetables were grown in the West of Ireland in those days: nobody ate them. But one farmer had, for some unknown reason, planted a bed of leeks. Could I buy some? No. 'But just work away — help yerself whenever ye feel like it. We don't eat 'em — got no use for 'em.' Someone dumped a load of peat, what they call turf in Ireland, outside my door. They did let me pay them a few shillings for this. I don't think you would find this sort of generosity in the west of Ireland today: too many tourists have gone there. (I was there perhaps thirty-five years ago.) The generosity I received was the generosity of poor people; these people had very little but were liberal with what they had. They had not really developed a money-based economy yet, but they have now.

One day I walked far up into the mountains. It was a rare fine day; the sun was shining and the larks were singing. I found a young man digging peat on an upland peat bog. We passed the time of day — he seemed very eager to rest on his loy and talk.

'I envy you, working up here on the mountain with the larks singing about you,' I said.

'Well, 'tis the last time I'll be doing it.'

'Why?'

'My brother works in England — Northumberland. He drives a mechanical digger. It'll pick fifty tons of coal up with one swipe! How is it I can go on diggin' away here with this spade that'll only pick up an ounce!'

'How many days a year do you have to dig turf to keep your home warm?'

'Oh, two, three weeks.'

'And what does your brother earn in a week?'

He told me, and I worked out that with the price of coal his brother had to buy, it took that man a month out of every year to keep his house warm. 'So you're getting the better of him,' I said, 'and you can hear the larks sing while you work. Your brother can't.'

But I'm sure that he did go off to join his brother, and enlist in the great army of uprooted Irish exiles in England who want to participate in a money-based economy.

On another occasion, an old man accosted me in a lane. 'You're a writer I hear,' he said.

'For my sins.'

'Ye'd be interested — I had a writer for a customer. I'm a tailor. I made his suits.'

'What's his name?'

'Oh you'd never be after hearing of him, he's dead now. He was much older than you are. Look, come to my house and I'll show you a few things might amuse ye.'

We strolled along to a remote thatched cabin on a hillside. The little house was practically bare inside. There were two cheap wooden chairs, an open turf fire with a black pot over it, and near it a low wooden platform, upon which my host was wont to sit, cross-legged, while he sewed his cloth. He was a bachelor, and needed no more than he had.

He had a little drawer, with no chest to put it in, and this he held out to me. 'You being a writer might be interested,' he said. 'This man came here on a bike. He asked me to make him a suit, so I did. And it had to be cut strange — Norfolk shooting jacket he was after calling it. He never came again; used to send me a postcard when he wanted another, with sometimes a slight change of measurements on it.' The little drawer was full of these postcards. They were all signed 'George Bernard Shaw'.

I made great friends with the tailor, and often used to go and sit in his cabin and talk to him. He was a thinking man and a philosopher, but he did not read much (in fact there was nothing in his cabin for him to read), and I am quite sure that he did not know that his client was in any way famous.

'Look,' I told him. 'One day some stranger is going to come into this house and offer you a fiver for those postcards. Don't take it! They're worth a hell of a lot more than that.' But I don't know whether he believed me, nor what happened to them.

Well, I wanted to see my old tailor again, so Angela and I set out from Glengarriff along the magnificent coast road to the west and then up, up, high into the Caha Mountains. Rough, barren mountains they were. The road took us over a high pass which has a great crucifix at the top of it. From the summit we looked down the famous Heeley Pass, at a view of cosmic splendour — a great lake below us, the sea beyond, and mountains beyond that — and then wound down steeply on to the low land bordering Kenmare River, as that bay is oddly called.

Quite suddenly we were in lush country with thick woodlands and rhododendrons. Then we came to the small salt-water inlet that Kilmakilloge is on and I saw O'Sullivan's Bar. 'Teddy O'Sullivan' was written over it in beautiful Irish script. I didn't recognize it — I didn't recognize anything. Thirty-five years is a hell of a long time. But the landlord was the same, and he actually remembered my short residence all those decades ago. I asked him about the tailor.

'The tailor?' he said. 'Oh, you're talking of the Tailor of Kerry. Yes, he's gone now, may he rest above.'

He told me that the Tailor became quite famous. The local paper had found out about the postcards and published articles about them and their owner, and ever after that, until he had died, the Tailor was often in the news. 'And he died a very rich man.' Apparently he had been wont to travel over the mountains into County Cork once a week to sell clothes to the farmers there, and, because he didn't spend anything, had amassed a great deal of money, which he obviously couldn't take with him when he died. I was saddened to hear that he was gone for he was an unusual individual. May God rest his soul.

We drove back to Glengarriff through several tunnels that Thackeray drove through a hundred and sixty years ago, and we shouted as we went, as no doubt Thackeray did.

CHAPTER SIXTEEN

~

The City of the Broken Treaty

HEN I WAS TRAVELLING IN IRELAND for the first time, alone, I slept in a bed and breakfast house in a small town somewhere in the West (I don't remember where), and there was a creamery just over the road. From six in the morning, and then on for several hours, a slow-moving queue formed leading to the creamery: a bizarre procession of horses and carts, asses and carts, tractors pulling small trailers, and occasional old bangers of motor cars. All these vehicles carried milk churns. Their drivers patiently waited their turn, had their milk weighed and poured down a conduit, got a fresh churn, and then trotted off whence they had come. I reflected that if they had come any real distance most of their working day must have been taken up with this operation. I wanted to lean out of the window and shout to them: 'Make your own cheese and butter! Sell that! Why should this creamery here have all the VAT? In far less time than it takes you to bring your milk in here and drive home again you could do all your own cheese- and butter-making.' I did not shout this of course, and if I had I doubt they would have taken any notice of me.

But subsequently, when Angela and I were travelling round, near Gougane Barra, the holy place, we saw a young, very hairy man leading half a dozen goats. Or were they leading him? They probably thought so. He proved to be a young Dutch settler who, with his wife, milked forty goats up in some rugged, rocky country that was fit for very little else, and made a very delicious cheese with the milk. We bought some and, compared to the cheese made in big factories, it was like a good deed in a naughty world. We have met a lot of new settlers such as these, mostly Dutch or German, who have moved into the West.

When we were driving along the shore of Bantry Bay we came to a small inn with a steep garden beside it laid out in 'lazy beds', or raised beds, and closely planted with small brassica plants. Just beyond there was a road junction, and by it stood two rugged-looking, mountain-faring men. One had a car, with two milk churns in it; the other a donkey cart, with the same. There were two stainless-steel mobile milk tanks stationed permanently by the side of the road; these would be emptied into the big tanker-lorry when it came. This is the new way of milk collection from remote small farms.

I stopped and asked the men what the little brassica plants were in the nearby garden. 'Cabbages' one said. 'They'll be planted out next April.' This was a considerable advance, I thought. No-one would have thought of growing cabbages, or any other form of green vegetable, in the West of Ireland when I first went there thirty-five years ago; except, that is, the professional gardeners of a few big estates. The traditional diet was soda bread, milk, butter-milk, eggs, butter, potatoes, fish occasionally, and mutton sometimes. But, if you think about it, in a countryside of few or no fences, where sheep roam where they will, it is very hard to keep a garden, and there was no tradition of it. With the influx of so many tourists though, and the consequent opening of shops that sell vegetables, these ideas are slowly changing. But whether home production in Ireland will be able to withstand the competition of fruit, vegetables, and anything else flooding in from every other country of Europe remains to be seen.

Back on our travels, we hitched up and drove in the direction of Limerick. We wanted to avoid steep hills, and so drove north to Kenmare (admittedly over some fairly steep terrain), but then we made for the Blackwater Valley and drove east along it. The general lie of the land in southern Ireland is a series of parallel mountain ranges, all running east to west. The rivers — the Nore, the Suir, the Blackwater, the Lee and the Bandon — all rise in the west and have been constrained by these waves of mountains to run more or less due east for nearly the whole of their courses. Then, as if they begin to despair of ever getting out to the sea, they suddenly make a dramatic turn southwards, breaking through the mountain range to the south of them, and quickly reach the sea. The Blackwater does this. We joined it near its source and travelled eastward along a green and fertile valley: real fattening pasture by the look of it. Angela found this landscape

145

dull after the dramatic and theatrical country we had lately been in, but I reflected that if I were still a farmer I would far prefer a hundred acres of this than a thousand of the other. The farmsteads looked comfortable and prosperous. We drove through the little town of Mallow, which had at one time been a fashionable resort for wealthy landowners. There was a spar there in the eighteenth century for fashionable hypochondriacs, with assembly rooms and all the rest of it.

North we went, through a valley between the Ballyhoura and the Mullaghareirk Mountains, to the great fertile alluvial plain south of Limerick. People imagine that the whole of the West of Ireland is barren and rugged, but in fact much of it is gentle and very fertile plain. But the tourists don't go to those places; they prefer the barren ones.

They do go, though, to the beautiful and most interesting village of Adare (*Ath Dara*, the Ford of the Oak), and we went there too, but you would need at least a day to see it properly. There are no less than three ruined monasteries there (in case one would not be enough), plus a large castle, a huge manor house, a number of beautiful thatched cottages, the Dunraven Arms Hotel and God knows what else. When one of the monasteries — the Augustinian Priory — was destroyed by Henry VIII, the forty-five friars who lived there were, quite simply, put to death. But if you love ruins, Henry VIII should be your favourite man, for he, or his hirelings, made many of them: probably more than Cromwell.

The Earls of Dunraven, who owned the place, have been generous: the First Earl gave the Trinitarian Priory to the Catholic Church (which built it in the first place); and the Third Earl gave the Fever Hospital, wanted no more for its original purpose, to the Christian Brothers as their school. The Christian Brothers, incidentally, are widespread all over Ireland, running boys' schools which have a reputation for high scholastic attainment and stern discipline.

The castle at Adare is called Desmond Castle, after the Earls of Desmond who once lived there, the Geraldines, or Fitzgerald family, whom we have met before. (A massive book could be written about the Fitzgerald family in Ireland, and it would read like an historical romance of Sir Walter Scott — multiplied a few thousand times!) One branch of the family, that of Kildare, had this castle at Adare and yet another nearby at Croom. So Irish were they that even their war cry was Irish: *Croom Abu!* which apparently means 'Croom to Victory!' We went to Croom, not to see the castle but to find out if anybody there remembered the famous Poets of Croom, the *Fili na Maighe* (Maighe is the river there). In the eighteenth century, the village was apparently a veritable nest of singing birds. They wrote in Irish, and they invented the limerick (Croom of course is in County Limerick). Besides limericks they wrote much serious verse, which has since been published in two volumes: *Fili na Maighe* and *Eigse na Maighe*.

Angela, who is learning Irish, was very interested in all this, so off we went to the village. On going into a pub, neither the landlord nor the few customers there had the slightest knowledge of the Maighe poets and had never even heard of them. This is sad because one of the poets at least was a publican, and wrote the following limerick, here translated into the English by Mangan:

> *I sell the best brandy and sherry*
> *To make all my good customers merry.*
> *But at times their finances*
> *Run short as it chances,*
> *And then I feel very sad, very.*

Let us only hope it was better in the original Irish; but that's as near as we ever got to the bards of the River Maighe.

I didn't want to go to Limerick city. I hate big towns, and had heard bad reports about Limerick from quite a lot of people. But Angela insisted that we go there: she wanted to see for herself. It was sunset when we arrived, and our road, from the south, brought us straight into the main road, O'Connell Street. We quickly came to a magnificent crescent with a statue of Daniel O'Connell the Liberator in it. There was an air of great civility about the place, all built, one would imagine, by wealthy merchants towards the end of the eighteenth and beginning of the nineteenth centuries. Limerick is built at the head of the Shannon Estuary, and is, as it always was, a seaport. Like Dublin, it was founded by the Vikings, and one can see why they chose the site: it's on a navigable river in the heart of fertile and most fruitful land.

We threaded through the city (it would be a town in most countries, it is quite small) and drove north to find a caravan site at O'Brien's Bridge, between the Shannon and the canal. Next day we went back to Limerick, and spent a lot of time wandering around it; during the next few days we got to know it very well. It is a lively town, with an active cultural and artistic life. We went to one play there, at the arts centre, called *Poor Beast in*

147

the Rain, an excellent production, written about our very own Wexford town by a Wexford man, Billy Roche. Our several days walking round Limerick were not long enough to get to know anybody very well, but long enough to get the flavour of the place. We both found it a most likeable town.

I have two great Irish heroes, both very different kinds of men. One was Michael Davitt, the land reformer, whom we shall meet in due course; the other was Patrick Sarsfield, a soldier and cavalry leader. Davitt was a teetotaller, but my guess is that Sarsfield was nothing of the kind. He was a rip-roarin', hard-ridin', swashbucklin' cavalier, a cavalry leader of the very first grade — at least the equal of Prince Rupert — and furthermore a man of chivalrous principles, a man who if he gave his word would not go back on it no matter how enormous the temptation to do so. It was this latter trait that was to prove the undoing of the Irish cause after the Treaty of Limerick was signed.

Sarsfield had joined James II's army in France. James thought him 'not very intelligent', but nevertheless sent him to Ireland to reorganize the royal army there. (James, of course, had fled from England the moment William of Orange had set foot there.) Sarsfield had a cavalry command at the Battle of the Boyne, but either jealousy or stupidity on the part of his superiors did not permit him to conduct the campaign as he wished. If he had charged the enemy at the crucial moment when they were in disarray after having forded the Boyne, he would have taken them from the flank and no doubt completely rolled them up. It was not Sarsfield who was 'not very intelligent', it was his commanders.

After the Boyne, and after King James had deserted his army and scuttled away to France, the Irish commanders decided to fall back on Limerick and hold the line of the River Shannon; they still had high hopes of French aid coming in time to save them. William of Orange's forces followed them and took up positions to the east of the city, where they waited for the artillery train to catch up. When it did, they had no doubt they could easily storm Limerick. 'The great grey guns' would always prevail against those who had none of them.

But Patrick Sarsfield prevailed upon his French commanders to let him have a go at intercepting the guns. He took six hundred hand-picked horsemen and, guided by a colourful character named Galloping O'Hogan, he led them out of Limerick, by the back door as it were. Taking a very circuitous route to fool the enemy, he forded Lough Derg at a place where that lake (which is part of the River Shannon) was fordable, made an epic

148

ride through the Silvermine Mountains and Slieveflim, and caught up with William's siege train at a place called Ballyneety. He attacked it, taking the defenders completely by surprise. No doubt killing those of them who did not surrender or run away, he filled the cannon up with gun powder and buried them muzzle-down in the ground, piled wagons and other equipment on top of them and blew the whole lot of it sky-high! It was one of the most completely successful commando raids in history.

Then came the difficult part, getting back. A troop of dragoons caught up with Sarsfield's rearguard and killed sixteen of them; but the others, with the 400 horses they had captured, all got back safely to Limerick.

What a superb guerrilla commander Sarsfield would have made. But this was not to be, for Ireland had simply become the cockpit of northern Europe. Most of the world looked upon these wars between the Jacobites and William as part of the wider struggle between Louis XIV and the great Protestant confederation of north-east Europe; the Irish were merely pawns. But Sarsfield's raid delayed the Franco-Hibernian defeat for another year. The Williamite army tried again to storm Limerick, this time without their guns, and failed. Winter was coming on, and the Irish-Protestant, English, Dutch, German and Danish troops with him began to melt away. William himself went back to England to look after his new kingdom.

But a year later William came back again, this time with guns. After winning several battles elsewhere he made another attack on Limerick, and this time persuaded the defenders to surrender. Then came the famous Treaty of Limerick. Angela and I stood by the Treaty Stone, near the Thomond Bridge on the Shannon, and took each other's photograph. But the treaty itself was less enduring than the stone it was signed on. Limerick is now known as 'The City of the Broken Treaty'. Sarsfield and the other commanders offered to talk terms, and signed a treaty which allowed for all those on the Irish side to decide for themselves whether they would go over to William's army or sail away to exile in France; it also promised religious freedom for Catholics. On 5 October 1691 the royal standards of England and France were set up on a hill outside the city. The Irish army marched out, and of the fourteen thousand men in it only one thousand and forty-six men chose the flag of William; the rest opted for France.

Two weeks later a large French fleet sailed up the Shannon, with plentiful reinforcements, supplies and ammunition. With all this, Sarsfield could have defeated William's army, and Ginckel, the Dutch commander of the Protestant forces, naturally assumed that Sarsfield would tear up the treaty and go on with the fight. But no. 'Ireland's honour is pledged,' he exclaimed. 'Though one hundred thousand Frenchmen offered to aid us now, we must keep our word!' He ordered the French fleet back to France, and he and all those who had opted for France sailed away with them to take service under the French king. 11,000 soldiers in all sailed to France. Sarsfield was killed two years later at the battle of Landen in the Low Countries. His last words were: 'If only this could have been for Ireland.' Of course, the Williamites immediately broke every clause of the treaty of Limerick that they had signed, and savage laws were passed against Catholics. The true Protestant ascendancy was now really born.

Naturally all this is the stuff of legend and romance; it fuels Irish patriotic fervour, just as does the story of the thirteen apprentice boys of Derry shutting the city gates in the face of the Catholic army. There were brave deeds and heroism on both sides. The Irish could not fight pitched battles against English armies without arms from abroad, and the suppliers of these arms — France and Spain — let the Irish down in every case. It is not for nothing that a later group carrying on the fight for Irish freedom called itself Sinn Fein, which means 'Ourselves Alone'.

It is an amusing, if useless, occupation to rewrite history but it can offer some insight into the different ways of understanding events. And I can claim with truth that I do not study and assess the wars of long ago as an 'armchair strategist'. I have been involved in wars; I fought in one, in the infantry, for six years, and during that time saw a great deal of active service in both Africa and Burma. I can write with some authority on, for example, guerrilla tactics, for I commanded the guerrilla platoon of my battalion when it had one, and most of the battles that I was involved in were really guerrilla battles. It is my belief that small oppressed nations can learn from the mistakes of the seventeenth-century Irish: do not try to fight pitched battles against the better-armed armies of the occupying power or form alliances with other great powers, (they will let you down every time), but adopt guerrilla tactics.

And so we moved on from Limerick, to wander round that strange lost world, the Burren, in County Clare, a huge desert of carboniferous limestone. Yet it is not quite a desert, for the flat limestone is fissured with grykes, deep, narrow clefts in the rock, and inside these, strange plants grow. They root in the soil that forms in the cleft, and are able to grow protected from the almost incessant Atlantic wind. The botany of the country is known world-wide, for here southern (Lusitanian) flora meet with northern (Hibernian), and plants exist that you would be hard put to find anywhere else. There is grass in places too, and moss — even up on top of the steep-sided hills and on the level terraces up the side there is grass. If you look up at these hills from below they are just barren limestone; if you look down at them from above they are grass. Strangely, the traditional practice elsewhere of summering the cattle on the tops of the hills and bringing them down for the winter is reversed here. The hills act as heat stores and the grass actually grows better on them in the winter than in the summer.

We wandered around this astonishing never-never land, finding everywhere the traces of early man: Neolithic and Mesolithic stone tombs; Iron-Age forts; early Celtic Christian buildings; churches and crosses (some of them works of high art); and more recent castles and towers. There are, amazingly, a few farmhouses still, inhabited with people actually farming them. Their cattle look fat and healthy as the grass, where it does occur, is good grass; limestone is healthy for man and beast.

The Burren is absolutely peppered with the ruins of Neolithic monuments; the place must have been highly populated four or five thousand years ago. In the few places where there are peat bogs, if you dig down through the peat you will find buried field systems, stone walls built by ancient men around their fields. My own belief is that the people who built all these destroyed the soil. Pollen analysis shows that the area was forested after the last Ice Age had retreated. I believe those early people cut all the trees down and stocked the area too heavily for them to come back again; so the soil disappeared leaving a barren desert where, as a Cromwellian soldier complained, 'there is not a tree big enough to hang a man, water enough to drown him, or earth enough to bury him.' To one of his profession a sore deprivation no doubt.

Because of Angela's inordinate love of the work of the poet Yeats we drove down off the Burren into the lush fertile plain to the east, and went to Coole Park, where the poet used to stay with Lady Augusta Gregory (who fancied poets much as other people fancy canaries). The mansion where they stayed was sold to the Irish government in 1928 and they could find nothing better to do with it than pull it down. But we wandered about the beautiful grounds and woods which remain — quite magical — and saw the copper beech tree on which G.B.S., Sean O'Casey, Yeats and other literati had carved their names; then we drove around a most beautiful lake where Yeats was wont to wander. Angela was learning to drive at the time and I think she was beginning to feel the first flush of overconfidence. She propelled our old banger along this narrow lane between the lake and steep woods at a furious speed. Suddenly we both saw a lone figure standing at the side of the lane, a surprising sight in such a completely unpopulated place. It was a young man — a young man, we both thought, who looked like he might well be a poet. (Indeed, who but a poet would be wandering in this beautiful but remote place?) Yes, he even looked like . . . No, it couldn't be! We had stood beside Yeats's grave only the day before, and read the short and cryptic message on it . . . SPLASH! We hit, full-on, a pool of water across the lane at least two feet deep. Angela had to concentrate on steering of course, but I was able to see, through that great wave of water that completely enveloped us, that it had completely enveloped our poet too; through the streaming rear window of the car I saw a young man as thoroughly drenched as if he had been standing underneath Niagara Falls.

'Oh God, shall we stop?' said Angela.

'No, drive on — drive on,' I said, most basely. But what could we have done?

And the epitaph on Yeats's grave:

> 'Cast a cold eye on life, on death,
> Horseman pass by.'

CHAPTER SEVENTEEN

~

One of the (Many) Islands of Saints and Scholars

T HE FIRST TIME I EVER WENT to Galway city was about 1960, some time after I had made the governess car trip around County Wexford, when the BBC asked me to return to Ireland with a tape recorder and make a few radio programmes for them. I was leaning on a railing looking down at a small boat on a stream which flowed into the harbour below. A voice with a strong American accent surprised me.

'D'ye know what kind of a vessel that is?' it said.

I turned to see a stocky, middle-aged man, who looked exactly like a typical American businessman.

'Well, I think it's a *púcán*,' I said.

'You're dead right. You sound like an Englishman?'

'I am.'

'Then how come you know what a *púcán* is? Kind of strange thing for an Englishman to know?'

'Read about 'em in a book; I'm interested in working sailing craft. And how come you know what they are? You're an American aren't you?'

He pointed vaguely westward. 'There's an island out to sea there,' he said. 'Inishmore, one of the three Aran Islands. I was born there.'

Now my idea of the Aran Islands was formed by having seen that classic film *Man of Aran* as a child, and having read Synge's book on the islands. This caused me to imagine that the islanders were all rugged, tough seamen, but the man I was talking to looked anything but that; he looked like a typical middle-aged small-town American businessman. But he went on discussing the *púcán*, and describing the larger members of the Galway Hooker tribe:

the *gleoiteog* and the *bad mor*, and also the little canvas-covered *currachs* that the men of the west coast of Ireland use for fishing and other purposes. 'I was brought up in 'em,' he said. 'Many's the time I've been out in weather you wouldn't believe. If a man don't know what he's doing, they're death-traps.'

He told me he was going back to the island after twenty years away from it, and his name was John Mullen. He was going to see his old widowed mother and his brother who lived in the same house. He had his wife with him, but she was American born and bred and he didn't know if she could stand the primitive conditions on the island.

'Will you stay over there?' I asked.

'Maybe I would if I was on my own; I don't think she will though.'

'She' was shopping, so we moved on to a pub. When he heard that I was just drifting around looking at the country he suggested I come over to the island with him. I could stay in the house where his mother and brother lived. 'She speaks no English but you'll get on fine with her just the same.' In the event, I did.

We boarded the ferry in due course, a large motor-trawler, fitted out, I was glad to see, with a bar. Here we settled ourselves, and my new friend told me stories of his life on the island many years ago. I remember one, rather silly story about how they used to smuggle Spanish brandy and other substances ashore from the fishing trawlers that used to come and fish the grounds there. He went out in the family *currach* with his brother and another boy to sell some lobsters to a trawler that was anchored off the island. (There were lobsters aplenty in those days, he said. Now, because of overfishing, they were scarce.) They took some empty bottles with them in the hope of filling them up, but there was nothing doing — the trawlermen were either out of the stuff or else fearful of the law. 'I guess on the way back I just took one of these bottles and filled it up with sea water. When we hit the beach there was this old boy — great boozer — and he shouted, 'Get anything?' I handed him the bottle and he took a great swig of it: he swallowed half. You should have seen his face!'

We hove to off each of the two smaller islands of the three, Inishmaan and Inisheer. *Currachs* were awaiting bobbing on the quite large waves (an easterly was blowing), to take aboard mail and one or two passengers for the ferry. (This was the only way most of them had of getting to and from the mainland.) The men in the *currachs* handled their feather-light craft with skill. One heavy package was lowered into one *currach* containing, I should guess, a generator. Drums of oil and paraffin were also lowered aboard. The passengers, most of them women, had to be pretty agile to leap from the bobbing craft to the deck of the trawler. I thought how unsuitably dressed the women were for this sort of work; they were clad as for the city pavement.

We docked on the biggest island, at Kilronan, where there was an artificial harbour. Some men were engaged on building a stone monument on the quay. I asked what it was and they told me it was a monument to the two young English soldiers who had recently rowed across the Atlantic (the first people ever to do so), and set ashore at Kilronan. There was some controversy about it. Some of the islanders were averse to the idea of commemorating a feat achieved by English soldiers, but most were thoroughly in favour of it. 'They're after doing a great deed no matter who the hell they are,' said one of the builders.

A tractor with a trailer came down to the quay and took our luggage. Mine consisted of a portable tape recorder and a small haversack, but Mrs Mullen had enough to fill the whole trailer. We followed the tractor out of the tiny stone village on foot and crossed a stony and treeless landscape until we came to a house which was somewhat larger than most of the others scattered about the limestone plain. Here we were greeted by Dara Mullen, John's brother, and their old mother, a delightful lady as completely devoid of English as I was of Irish but with whom I had no difficulty in conversing.

I stayed with this family a few days, and they were consistently hospitable and kind to me. Dara was a farmer and a fisherman; and I remember when his brother — the successful American businessman — asked him the question, 'Are there many unemployed on the island?' Dara thought for a while before answering. 'There is nobody employed. We all work hard, and we make a good living; but nobody is employed, as such.'

There is nobody employed! What a marvellous thing it would be, I thought, to live in a world where nobody was employed. And, as I began to see how the island worked, I realized that nobody had to be employed. Everyone had access to some arable land, and to some grazing. True, both gave the appearance, at first sight, of being nothing but naked limestone; but then one realized that there were soil-covered patches here and there with magnificent green grass on them, and that the cattle, of which there were plenty, all seemed fat and healthy. On many points along the north-east coast, which was low and punctuated by plenty of small bays and inlets, I saw *currachs* lying bottom-up on the beaches. Near the houses and settlements there were small patches of soil shaped into 'lazy beds'. This soil was made by the islanders themselves, by mixing together sand and seaweed carried up from the shore. Aided by the climate, it grows the most magnificent potatoes. In places there were oats, too, enough to feed the population. Most of the houses were cabins built with randomly hewn stone (the limestone cleaves easily to make good building material), and many were roofed with thatch. Knowing what an expensive job thatching is in England, I was puzzled how people could afford it, until I met an elderly man in the pub who told me. He was a nice, gentle old man, and he told me he was the island thatcher, the one and only. His name was Jimmy Foley.

'What do you charge to thatch a roof?' I asked him.

'Nothing,' was his reply. 'Sure they keeps me in grub, and a few bottles of stout. I just does it to help people.'

In truth, the style of thatch was quite unlike English thatch. The straw (oat straw) was laid on ear-ends out and the thatch was very thin. Where English thatch, with wheat straw, may last thirty or forty years (and with Norfolk reed, seventy), this would need re-doing every two or three years. But if it only cost a few bottles of stout, what of it? My old thatcher, Jimmy Foley — a thirsty chap — told me of the days when he used to travel to Lancashire to work on English farms during the harvest or other busy seasons and he was amazed because they made him sleep in stables and out-houses. 'And them in great mansions, like palaces!'

In that same pub I met a strange old couple. The man was thin and hawk-faced, and had obviously been handsome once; his lady had no doubt been a beauty. They both spoke, unmistakeably, like actors, and actors they were. His real name was Michael Koffy, but he went under the stage name Jimmy Stone. ('I don't suppose there's a place in Ireland they don't know me — Jimmy Stone.') She said her name was Dolly Downes but he corrected her with some severity. '*Dorothy* Downes,' he said.

We drank some stout together, and then they suggested we go back to their house — a one-room cabin with an earth floor, one large double bed and a couple of packing cases by way of furniture — to drink some more, for the pub was closing. We took a decent supply of bottled stout with us. A slight difficulty was caused by the fact that we had only two drinking vessels, two chipped enamelled mugs, between the three of us, but I was quite happy to drink out of the bottle. A huge and very fat spaniel had constantly to be lifted up on to the bed, and off again, as he demanded, which was often. His heart, I was told, was not as strong as it was, and the strain of jumping either up or down was too much for him.

My host and hostess told me an extraordinary tale. Michael, who did most of the talking, had been a young fellow in County Cork, and had seen an advertisement in a local paper: Young man wanted for theatrical act. He answered it, and found that the advertiser was a large lady ('Very beautiful, but there was a lot of her!') who was looking for a young man to dress up as an Indian and festoon her with snakes. 'And me mortally afraid of serpents! I told her I could never do it, I was mortally afraid. But she stuck a couple of whiskies into me — "You'll do it fine when you have to, in front of the audience." And there I was on the stage in front of a lot of people, and she displaying her ample charms – she had very little on, but plenty of bangles and things. And there was this great wooden chest, and I had to open it and pull out these huge serpents and drape 'em round her, and then she did a sort of snake dance with 'em, which was a run-away success. And that night I had to sleep in the caravan with her — we travelled you see, on the road — and didn't all the snakes escape in the middle of the night and slither all over the place, with me runnin' around grabbin' them up, mortally afeared! But I got used to it, got to think nothing of it.'

As they travelled the roads of Ireland the showman bug bit deep into him, and he eventually left the serpent lady and went off with a company of touring players. 'There was this grand actor of the old school,' he told me, 'and he taught me to en-un-ci-ate perr-fect Eeng-lish. He was a great teacher and he wouldn't stand for slovenliness, in dee-ction or anything else.'

He travelled the roads with this group of players for many years, playing good theatres in provincial towns and cities, in Ireland, England, Scotland and Wales. Then he met Dorothy. 'She had been a fine actress on the legitimate stage,' he said. 'She was right at the top.'

'But I had fallen on hard times,' she put in, 'and had to take to the road. But I don't regret it, not one minute of it. I had a marvellous life.' Her accent was that of an educated English woman. 'And then I met your man here,' she said, evidently having picked up some Irish-isms. 'We moved in together and we've been old troopers together ever since.'

'What sort of parts did you play?' I asked.

'Oh, scores of 'em. Melodramas mostly. You know, The Murder in the Red Barn, Wuthering Heights. He was Heathcliff, I was Cathy . . .'

'I have come back here Cathy — I had to come back!' he declaimed.

'You had no right to come back. What is past is gone and can never, never be again.'

'No, Cathy, you're wrong. You're mine — you'll always be mine. You love me in your heart and soul. But come, Cathy, and let me take you to the window. It's a glorious moonlit night.'

'Yes, Wuthering Heights in all its glory — it's sometimes shrouded in dense mists — Wuthering Heights, where we played together as children. Oh Heathcliff, those were the happiest days of our lives.'

'The happiest days, Cathy, when we played as girl and boy and you pledged yourself to me and I to you for all eternity' . . .

It was the cinema that eventually broke the travelling players, first the silents, then the talkies finished the job. 'It got harder and harder to find a stage in a proper theatre,' explained Michael. 'We started having to go to more and more remote places, the Outer Hebrides, tiny remote places. Many's the time we played on stages built up on fish barrels; we've even had the stage collapse under us!'

They told me marvellous stories, like how once, in County Cork, they put up in the digs they always did, but didn't have enough money to pay the landlady. They climbed out of the bathroom window in the small hours and slid down a drainpipe to escape. But the second from last fugitive to leave — and the fattest — got stuck. The man behind pushed him and the one outside pulled, but to no avail. He was a very Falstaff. Finally they had to bang on the front door and wake the landlady; and together they unstuck the man.

'Oh what are ye talkin' about!' she exclaimed. 'Yiz didn't have to do that! Glory be to God, if yiz couldn't pay I'd have said nothin' about it and given yiz a fiver for your next journey. Haven't we known each other long enough? Don't be so bloody stupid. Get back to bed the lot of ye and I'll gi' yiz a good breakfast in the mornin'!'

Another time, when one of their number died, they couldn't afford an undertaker, so they got a man with a small truck to carry their deceased colleague. Then followed some terrible tale of both the truck carrying the coffin and they themselves getting lost; they were all in different pubs. But eventually, as happens in Ireland, everybody got together again, the priest was found, and the body given a decent burial.

I asked them how they ended up on the Aran Islands. 'Sure, it got worse and worse,' said Michael, 'and we couldn't make even a few shillings. When we came to play Galway we got so little for it that the owner of the theatre — well, we couldn't pay him, so he locked the door and kept the scenery.'

And so that was the end of the little troupe which had carried on so valiantly — carried on a tradition that went back long before Shakespeare and should never never have died — killed by the celluloid stories imported from across the Atlantic. Some false idea of sophistication made honest country people think it was worth paying to go and watch this 'entertainment', when they wouldn't watch real actors in real plays.

Realizing that the long road had ended — the road of the real, living theatre — Michael and Dorothy bought an old cinema projector and just managed to pay the single fare over to Kilronan, where they earned a living showing films in the community hall. Now, even that was over, and they lived in their bare little cabin with just each other and their dog for company. The islanders loved them and were kind to them and gave them milk and fish and eggs, and no doubt they had some sort of (meagre) pension. When I came to leave them, I was sad but uplifted. I had enormous admiration for them — certainly for their unconquerable determination, but especially for their unfailing laughter and light-heartedness in the face of adversity.

I decided to walk the length of the island, which took just a day. The wind was blowing from the south-west, and when I approached the cliff edge on the south-west face of the island it nearly blew me over. The Aran Islands (a geological extension out into the sea of the Burren country we had already travelled through) have their highest edge facing the Atlantic, with a lofty vertical cliff falling straight into the sea below, and slope gently down to the opposite shore which is at sea-level. I had been warned that because of the updraught where the sou'-wester hits the vertical cliff there are often back-eddies which can suck you over the edge and hurl you into the sea. I therefore approached the edge with some caution. Then, after walking some way, I saw a figure sitting right on the edge of the cliff. I approached carefully, and found a twelve-year-old boy sitting with his legs dangling over the edge of the cliff fishing, with a very long line, in the water three hundred feet below him. He was doing very well too, regularly pulling up a wrasse, or rock fish. Such was the distance between him and the sea that it took him a long, long time to pull one up. I admired his sang-froid.

I cut inland after this. Picking my way over the rocky fields bounded by limestone walls, I had just come up to a huge boulder such as one often finds on the island (and on the Burren), when I was transfixed. I heard the most haunting and beautiful singing that I have ever heard coming from behind the great rock, and I stood there absolutely entranced, unable to move. It was not like any European singing I knew, and it was not in any scale that I knew, nor language either — it was pure Irish.

159

Then it stopped, and I walked round the rock. There was a little thatched cabin, and outside stood a stunningly beautiful teenage girl, washing clothes in a wooden tub. She didn't run away as I walked up to her, she understood the English I spoke to her. Her mother and father were out, but she seemed not the least abashed by me. I was lugging the BBC tape recorder and asked her if she would sing to me again. She agreed, and I recorded her. Her voice was no doubt heard by millions, but will never be heard by me again because the BBC kept the tape.

On I pressed. Rock and grey stone walls, more rock and grey stone walls, all enclosing tiny fields no bigger than a suburban lawn, and with no gates. I soon twigged that if you wanted to get cattle in or out of a field you simply pulled the wall down and built it up again. I had to climb over endless walls but was very careful not to dislodge a stone.

Reaching the north end of the island, I came across a surprisingly big house, a great block of a farmhouse with *two* storeys (almost unheard of here). I walked up to it, and heard a kind of shush-ing sound coming from an outhouse. I looked in and found a man threshing barley by bashing the sheaves on the edge of a big barrel. Later, I knew, he would take the grain out and winnow the chaff from it in the wind.

I got talking to him and found that his name was Sonny Hernon. He and his wife owned the big house and took in guests. He took me in to meet his wife and she very kindly asked me to lunch. Sonny didn't know who had built the house nor why. I talked farming to him and he said that there was a good living to be earned if you could keep a small herd of beef cattle on the island, as the island cattle fetched a good price in Galway market. Barley and oats grew well, and so did potatoes; and there were always fish. The people were healthy.

I walked on, across to the north-west end of the island, spat in the sea for good luck and started back.

CHAPTER EIGHTEEN

~

Return to Aran

I WENT BACK TO INISHMORE in the company of Angela in the autumn of 1990, thirty years after I had gone there first. We had been invited by an organization called *Aisling Arrainn*, which we took to be a kind of neo-Celtic Christian monastic order. There was to be a seminar presided over by the philosopher-priest Ivan Illich, and as we had read some of his books we were keen to meet him.

We were staying in our caravan not far from the tiny port of Rossaveal on the rocky coast of Connemara. The first day we drove there, the ferry to Aran was cancelled: it was a perfectly foul day, strong sou'-wester and raining like hell. The second day was not much better, but the captain decided to risk it, and aboard we went. The ferry was like nothing so much as a hefty steel tank. It had two mighty engines deep down in her belly, a sort of damp hole for such passengers as wished to get out of the weather, and an open after-deck which had some shelter afforded by the superstructure of the vessel. She certainly looked unsinkable, probably uncapsizable, and had obviously been designed and built for just the job she was doing.

We took our place on the after-deck, and the ferry steamed away from the dock. There were perhaps twenty people on deck, and as many again crammed down below. The wind made a rather direful sound screaming through the rigging above us. I noticed a very tall, thin, angular, quite old man, with a thin, aquiline face, bracing himself with his back against the after-rail. He seemed to be the centre of a party of friends and admirers. That, I thought, is Illich.

As long as we ran down the sheltered fiord the sea was calm, but as soon as we poked our nose out into the Atlantic things were very different. The ferry rolled like a pig, sheets of spray flew over us, and a considerable depth of water swilled about the deck. It was exhilarating.

The man I thought was Illich seemed to be enjoying it as much as I was. For about an hour we thumped and wallowed, and then as we came into the lee of Inishmore, our island, the sea was immediately calmer. When we docked in Kilronan Harbour the people issued from the hole below, some of them looking distinctly green.

Ashore we found a handsome young man dressed in a woollen hat and waterproofs, waiting to welcome us. He was Dara Molloy who, even if he was not the abbot, was at least one of the more permanent features of the community to which we were going. A minibus stood by, we all got in it — including my Ivan Illich who indeed proved to be the Ivan Illich, and half our fellow passengers from the boat, who also proved to be pilgrims like ourselves — and we drove southwards.

The community turned out to be a very informal affair: half a dozen people perhaps, men and women, who lived on the island in a loose-knit community. The *Aisling Arrainn* is a gallant attempt to found a sort of neo-Celtic Church community, but I think it makes a mistake in calling itself 'non-denominational'. Maybe if, in the past, the intelligent and innovative people who wished to reform the Church had stayed in it and tried to reform it from within, they would have done more good than they did by breaking away and setting up endless little sub-Churches of their own. To return to the values of the Celtic Church, as far as we can know them, would be a great thing. Liberation Theology is also a great thing, and must triumph; it must hang on in there and force the Church to accept its ideas, not just break away and form another little sect or sub-creed.

Dara Molloy and Tess Harper seemed to be much of the driving force behind this community (it is quite within the Celtic tradition for there to be both abbots and abbesses in the same community, monks and nuns too), but both of them would hate me to call them leaders of the community, though that is what they are, and without leaders no community can survive. They have two houses on Inishmore, some miles apart, and a little bit of land. They try very hard to produce their own food, and succeed quite well within the constraints of the land they have. They even have a *currach* and catch fish. They lead exemplary lives and make no great demands on the planet; they show much hospitality and encourage spiritual and intellectual discussion, hence luring Ivan Illich over from his lair in Mexico and inviting the rest of us to come and listen to him.

The house we stayed in was an enlarged farmhouse, one of the bigger houses on this island of small dwellings. Near it was a roofless Celtic

Christian church and the base of a round tower, both on land not owned, alas, by the community. I suggested to Dara Molloy that they should make it a long-term aim to restore both. If they did that they would become a virile and long-lasting community. I have great admiration for these people and would love to see them unashamedly take a Christian, nay a Catholic stance, and try to revive the Celtic Church traditions and revitalize the decadent European Christian Church from within. They should be in the forefront of the Liberation Theology movement, and maybe, who knows, they one day will be. God knows there is a need for it.

For three days we sat at Ivan Illich's feet (or rather he sat at ours, for he squatted on the floor wrapped up in a poncho while we perched on chairs), and I hope the other thirty or forty people who were there understood more of what he said than I did. But then, I am a very simple fellow and can easily be overawed by erudition.

And then it was Hallowe'en. Bands of children and some adults came knocking on the door, the children wearing gruesome masks and strange garments. They were all mute; none of them spoke one word. They were given nuts and fruit and cakes, and then wordlessly they went away. They were, we were given to understand, representing the dead, those people of the community who had gone before.

The *Aisling* held a great party that night. The one big room in the main house was crowded: there was the parish priest and other dignitaries; there were many local people, male and female, young and old; and there were those of us who had come to hear Illich, including a large family from somewhere in Ireland — father, mother, and five lovely children aged from twelve down to about two. The two-year-old could have been abominable (as two-year-olds generally are), crying and calling attention to itself when the local ladies were trying to sing their great Gaelic songs, but the older children took it upon themselves to quieten it (him or her — I cannot remember). It was obvious that this splendid family was united if necessary against the whole world; united as only a real human family can be; a group of people far more important and beautiful and valuable than simply the sum of its members.

Alas there were no musicians at the party, though many good singers, so a tape recorder was brought in to play some lively Irish music. The many local ladies present began to shout with one voice: '"The Siege of Ennis"! "The Siege of Ennis"!'

Now 'The Siege of Ennis' is a set dance of labyrinthine complexity;

it would take a giant computer to memorize all its intricate comings and goings, interweavings, swingings and turnings, changes of position and all the rest of it. Thank God, I thought, this lets me out. I shall sit quietly in this comfortable armchair and enjoy the intricate proceedings in peace.

But this was not to be. Twelve, as I shall call the pretty twelve-year-old girl who was the oldest child of the happy family I have described, rushed towards me with wild abandon, seized me by the belly of my beautiful Aran sweater, which Angela had only recently bought as a present for me, and dragged me to my feet. Now either I had to get up or my sweater would be irretrievably ruined. 'Dance! Dance!' she cried.

And dance I did. I had to, or I could see that beautiful sweater, with its cable stitches and plain and purl and all the rest of it, being turned back into the yarn from which it was knitted. I leapt and capered; I was hauled this way and that by my sweater, and was urged to ever more frenetic efforts by my small but active partner. No doubt we completely disrupted the entire proceedings, this fairy dancing with a hippopotomas, but I have to admit I thoroughly enjoyed it.

Now one cannot write of Ireland without a mention of the extraordinary part that the Irish played in the re-Christianizing of Europe, when the flame of European civilization had been all but extinguished during the Dark Ages. Dara Molloy has spoken and written very learnedly on the subject of Celtic monasticism. I first encountered it and became aware of it in Northumberland, on Holy Island (Lindisfarne) and the Farne Islands, and afterwards felt its strong influence on Iona, in the Hebrides. Then, in Wales, I found that the whole country had once been the domain of Celtic saints. I have already mentioned one of them in this book, Saint Brynach, whose monastery was at Nevern, in Pembrokeshire, near my farm, and who used to sit and meditate on the top of Carn Ingli, from where I first saw Ireland. Nearly every village in Wales has its saint, who was merely the founder of, and abbot or abbess of, the local monastic settlement; the same phenomenon occurs in Ireland, Cornwall and Brittany. As Dara Molloy points out, these monasteries and convents (many in fact were foundations of mixed sex) were not places where monks or nuns retreated from the world and cut themselves off from it. They were open places, where young people could come and stay and learn before moving on, possibly to another such establishment, and eventually perhaps, when they had acquired sufficient wisdom and sanctity, founding communities of their own. This system seemed to work, because it survived a thousand years and spread all over Europe. Much is known about the communities, for they left copious written records and also (when the Vikings, and later Henry VIII and Cromwell, spared them) priceless works of craftsmanship and art. Cromwell's men spread right over Ireland — even to the Isles of Aran — and assiduously smashed every Christian work of art they could find. On Inishmore they pulled down the Church of Saint Enda and also the great round tower to build a fort with the stone. Nearly every one of Ireland's magnificent High Crosses was defaced; only here and there, where the people managed to bury one before Cromwell's men came, has one survived intact. But in the National Museum in Dublin there are a number of great treasures of Celtic Christian art and craftsmanship, and in the library of Trinity College, Dublin, one can go and see the Book of Kells. The Lindisfarne Gospels, the Book of Durrough, and other illuminated manuscripts survive to tell us of a glory that is gone. The Roman version of Christianity was bound to triumph in the end, because it operated in the realm of power politics, and it triumphed very early in England, at the Synod of Whitby in 664. Quoting from my *Companion Guide to the Coast of North East England*:

'Everything we can discover of Celtic Christianity shows it to have been a purer, less materialistic and less worldly religion than that of Rome, and, more importantly, it did not organize itself in a rigidly hierarchical system. Perhaps if we could have retained it, monasticism in England would not have reached that stage of temporal power and corruption that gave its enemies the excuse to destroy it in the reign of Henry VIII. Perhaps, who knows, if the Celts had prevailed the Scots and Welsh and English would have become united, the Danes would have been defeated, and the Battle of Hastings would have had a different outcome.'

(Though, as an old friend of mine in Suffolk used to say, if your aunt had had balls she would have been your uncle.)

But, the Synod of Whitby notwithstanding, the Irish and Welsh missionaries spread far and wide into Europe. It was from the eighth to the tenth centuries that Celtic Christianity spread most widely in Europe, and the most important and best documented sites of Irish foundations on the Continent are Cologne, Fulda, Ghent, Liège, Würzburg, Peronne, Cambrai, Mainz, Regensburg, Soissons, Laon, Trier, Vienna, Paris, Reims, Strasbourg, Verdun, Reichenau, Salzburg, Luxeuil, Rheinau, Auxerre, Berne, Saint Gall, Milan, Piacenza, Verona, Bobbio, Fiesole, Lucca, Rome, Tarento and Naples.

In the furthering of their cause, missionaries often underwent hard privations, even suffering martyrdom. We know that Saint Columbanus voyaged right up the Rhine with his band of monks, and the following poem, translated from the Latin, is often attributed to him. I too know the unrelenting strength of the current in the mighty Rhine, and the great labour of rowing a heavy boat against a tide, where even to pause to rub your nose means losing several yards, so this poem means a great deal to me:

> See, cut in woods, through flood of twin-horned Rhine,
> passes the keel, and, greased, slips over seas —
> > Heave men! And let resounding echo sound our HEAVE!

> The winds raise blasts, wild rain storms wreak their spite,
> but ready strength of men subdues it all —
> > Heave men! And let resounding echo sound our HEAVE!

> Clouds melt away and the harsh tempest stills,
> effort tames all, great toil is conqueror —
> > Heave men! And let resounding echo sound our HEAVE!

> Endure, and keep yourselves for happy things,
> ye suffered worse, and these too God shall end —
> > Heave men! And let resounding echo sound our HEAVE!

> Thus acts the foul fiend, wearing out the heart,
> and with temptation shaking inmost parts —
> > Ye men, remember Christ with mind still sounding HEAVE!

> Stand firm in soul and spurn the foul fiend's tricks,
> and seek defence in virtue's armoury —
> > Ye men, remember Christ with mind still sounding HEAVE!

> Firm faith will conquer all and blessed zeal,
> and the old fiend, yielding, breaks at last his darts —
> > Ye men, remember Christ with mind still sounding HEAVE!

> Supreme, of virtues King, and fount of things,
> He promises in strife, gives prize in victory —
> > Ye men, remember Christ with mind still sounding HEAVE!

So Ireland and Wales sent out the sparks that rekindled civilization in a Europe in which it had nearly been extinguished by the pagan East. Is it too much to hope that once again the Celtic genius — nearly exterminated but still smouldering away on the western seaboard of Europe — should fulfil the same purpose and strike out to combat the beastly materialism, the pagan money-worship, that has spread over the Western world like a deadly plague?

When we had had our fill of listening to people talk, Angela and I left the *Aisling* and struck out across the island, climbing out of one little field into another (being very careful not to dislodge any stones — I know the labour that goes into building dry stone walls), until we came to the mighty stone amphitheatre of Dun Duchathair. We could see, to the south-east, the other two islands of Aran (Inishmaan and Inisheer) and beyond them the mighty Cliffs of Moher, the highest vertical cliffs in Europe. We marvelled at the great stretches of bare limestone pavement, split with grykes, or fissures, in which grew strange and beautiful plants; we admired the gallant little trees that had germinated in these places and grown almost horizontally along the bare rock, never daring to rise more than a few inches above it.

The island has much changed. There are far more houses, most of them featureless modern bungalows that jarr with the rocky treeless landscape, and gone are the picturesque thatched cottages. The old lifestyle of self sufficiency has also been much eroded. Natives now earn their living by tourism and buy what they want from the mainland instead of producing it themselves. I should say the diet of the people is far worse and less nutritious than before; after all, with a regime of fish caught straight from the sea, oats and potatoes, and possibly some kale grown on that wonderful limestone soil, fresh unpasteurized milk from the island's cows, mutton from its sheep, how could people not be healthy? Now all food comes from the mainland, mostly in tins.

We dropped down into Kilronan (*Cill Rónáin*), where the ferry docks, and where there are three pubs. We went into one of them and quickly made friends with two men: one the village carpenter, who built most of the island's *currachs*; the other a fisherman-farmer, a fine-looking man with white hair, piercing blue eyes, and a clear complexion on a face that looked as though its owner had never known an evil thought. He wore a blue fisherman's jersey with a black suit over it and a black hat on his head.

I asked them about my friends the ancient actors, and they told me they were both dead. I had expected to hear this. John Mullen, the American

167

who had befriended me in Galway city all those years ago, was very much alive though, and his brother Dara was still around, working as the island's postman. I then learned something very interesting. The ferry service from Rossaveal had been founded by and owned by none other than John Mullen. In spite of his wife's misgivings about living on a small island he had, indeed, decided to stay on there, agitating for an airstrip to be established, with daily flights to and from the mainland, and putting up the money himself for the new ferry service from Rossaveal. He had been appalled by the fact that there was no employment on the island and had decided to remedy it. I remember him saying to his brother all those years ago that he wanted to start a restaurant at Kilronan to attract tourists and bring some money into the island. Now there is a daily influx, all summer, of hundreds of tourists — the population of the island suddenly more than doubles as tourists stream off the main ferry from Galway city. There are cars on the island now, too (I didn't see one when I was there before). I have no doubt that the beautiful teenager who sang the lovely song while she was washing the family clothes in the sunshine now has the latest automatic washing machine, and doesn't sing at all because she is listening to pop music on the radio. But who am I to say whether these changes are for the better or the worse? I don't live on a small island and I do have a washing machine.

Our two friends in the pub were consistently friendly, and kept trying to ply us with more drinks. We had a fight to keep our end up in this respect. I think they had expected us just to be the usual kind of tourists at first, but after they had found out that I had been on the island thirty years before and had known the Mullens and the Koffees they took more interest in us. They told us about life during the summer, when the island was absolutely flooded with tourists. 'The ferry from Galway docks, and they swarm ashore like ants,' said the fisherman. 'They swarm all over the place! They don't know what to do. Some of 'em try to crowd into the pubs but they can't all get in, so they swarm all over the island.'

'The people who stay a week or two or three are the best,' said the carpenter. 'Grand people, often; come here year after year. It's the day-trippers that we could do without.' And I could well understand the privation of being kept out of your own pub.

'We get some yobbos too, like football crowds. Some of 'em smashed the monument out there to the boys who rowed the Atlantic.'

They told us, too, that there is increasing demand on the island for a roll-on/roll-off ferry, not so much for the benefit of the tourists but for the

islanders who have cars and want to be able to drive about when they get
to Galway. To my mind motorcars should have no place on the island at
all. The island is only nine miles long and very narrow, and there is plenty
of horse-drawn transport — you can find hackney coachmen waiting every
day down at the harbour to drive tourists about.

But tourists are not the only problem. Though thirty years ago there
seemed to be a danger that these islands would be abandoned by their
inhabitants, now they are suffering from overpopulation. Too many people
are trying to crowd on them and build new houses; there is a serious problem
with sewage disposal on that porous limestone rock; and water is in short
supply, often polluted.

What a chance the islands have of adopting a really green solution to
their problems! The water supply problem could be eased if the sewage
problem was solved, for it is the pollution of underground water by sewage
that exacerbates the shortage. The sewage problem could be solved simply
and easily by constructing some methane, or biogas, digesters. Sewage that
goes into methane digesters gives up its methane, which can be profitably
burnt for useful purposes (thus preventing the methane from going up into
the stratosphere to add to the greenhouse effect), and the residual matter is
odourless, harmless, and a damned fine fertilizer. It could be used to build
up the islands' soils. Electrical energy could easily be provided by wave
power and wind power. (There is probably no more suitable site for this in
the world.) Cars could be banned, and a frequent minibus service shuttling
backwards and forwards the length of the island substituted. A positive
policy favouring home-produce would revive the islands' agriculture, trade
and industry and improve the health of the inhabitants. Using local material
for building (stone and thatch) instead of breeze blocks from the mainland,
would keep the money on the island as well as greatly improving its charm
and appearance. It might be none of my bloody business — and I'm sure
many of the islanders would be the first to say so — but I'm sure it is a
workable solution.

Back on the mainland, before going on to explore Galway city and
the Counties of Galway, Mayo and Sligo, we stayed at a little place called
Spiddal, or *An Spideal*, on the shore of Galway Bay west of Galway city. The
caravan site was half a mile back from the shore, surrounded by the rocks
that had been bulldozed out of the way to make room for the caravans. Ours
was the only occupied caravan there. We arrived in the evening, cooked and
ate a meal (a modern trailer caravan may not be very beautiful, it may not

be — indeed certainly is not — very romantic, but it is comfortable and convenient) and then we strolled down to Spiddal and the nearest pub. This was called Tighe Hughes, and when we walked in the place was swinging. There was a melodion player named Tim Ryan, a flautist, two tin whistle players, a guitarist, a banjo player and — last, but not least because she was so brilliant — a lady who played the spoons. Later, when she got up and began to dance, people immediately joined her and started a set. Spontaneous country dancing seems much more common in the West of Ireland than it is where we live, though the music in the West is no better than ours; if anything it is more self-conscious, because more under the scrutiny of tourists. (We have no tourists.) Foreigners crowd into the pubs just to hear, and learn to play, Irish music. One Bank Holiday, the pub in Spiddal was crowded out with Dubliners, and two Americans, a young girl and a boy. The girl tried to play the bodhrán and the bloke the tin whistle, both equally badly. But the musicians made room for them, and tried to teach them, and treated them with great patience and kindness. I am always amazed at how patient Irish country musicians are with beginners. The latter play hell with the music, but the older musicians suffer them and give them every encouragement. And how else can they learn? You can only learn real folk music by listening to it live and then joining in playing it; you cannot learn it from a book.

We spent much time exploring Galway city, the centre of which is pleasantly jumbled and has a medieval air to it, although few medieval buildings survive. In pre-railway days it and Limerick were important ports: anything the people of the West of Ireland wanted either to import or to export probably went through them. Galway certainly had an important trade with Spain and Portugal: most of the wine that the Anglo-Irish squirearchy used to quaff came into Galway. Trade with England too (mostly via Bristol) also came to Galway, and it must have been considerable. Galway was indeed a flourishing and important trading city, but the moment the railway came all this died. Suddenly Galway had the ground cut from under its feet. Henceforth, goods tended to pass through Dublin, transported by rail to and from the West of Ireland. Galway itself, fine city though it was, did not have much of a hinterland; it was left somewhat out on a limb and sank into a pleasant dreaming apathy. From this it has been aroused, in recent decades, by some kind of renaissance. It now has a very lively university, to which students come from all over the world, and a very cosmopolitan air about it. Various light industries have grown up with the help of central government. But above all there seems to have been a vigorous cultural revival.

There is a good arts centre, plenty of drama, a veritable plethora of traditional music, and altogether a feeling of great liveliness and cultural activity. It is in easy reach of Dublin, and many Dubliners seem to come there to try to rediscover their Irish roots.

The revival of Galway has inevitably led to a considerable influx of people from the surrounding country, and therefore huge sprawling suburbs to the north of the city, which are as unpleasant, to my eyes, as anything Dublin has to offer (which is quite something). Huge modern shopping complexes have sprung up, and it almost seems as if the residential areas which surround them are there simply to supply them with customers. We went into one of the very few small shops that has managed to survive in this human desert. It was fortified like a bunker, with thick concrete walls and tiny barred windows to fend off the sort of criminal attack which is almost inevitable in these human waste-lands. The estates have grown up far too quickly for there to be any organic growth, a centre, or centres, a tradition, a flavour, a sense of community, of belonging. They are just dumping places for uprooted humans. But far removed from all this is the true city of Galway, which is a pleasant, interesting and delightful place: one of the few cities in the world in which I would like to live.

CHAPTER NINETEEN

~~

We Stood by the Grave of
Michael Davitt

IN THE MEANTIME, THOUGH, I had to make do with my caravan at Spiddal, back along the Connemara coast. Connemara is a part of County Galway, which is part of the province of Connaught (*Cuige Chonnacht*). Tourists go to Connemara to see the amazing scenery, but to a farmer's eye it is a hell of a place, just a desert of random boulders. People have, with unimaginable labour, shoved and cajoled these huge boulders (some of them as big as a house) from where they were dumped by Ice-Age glaciers to make fields — all of them small, many of them minute, no bigger than a suburban front lawn. They grow grass, and because of the abundant rainfall it is lush grass (though not as nutritious as the Aran or Burren grass because the rock is not limestone) and some are dug up into lazy beds for potatoes.

When Cromwell's troops said 'To Hell or Connaught' for all those dispossessed Irish Catholics who could not find employment with Protestants they were not giving them much of a choice. Connaught was fully occupied, and refugees just had to fit in where they could. Hence the small holdings scattered everywhere, including those places utterly unfit for human settlement or survival.

Amazingly, the Cromwellian conquerors did not leave them alone even then. They followed them, and the whole of rocky Connaught, like the rest of Ireland, was carved up among English landlords, whose agents then turned to grinding whatever little bit of value they could from these refugees in a desert land. The Griffith Valuations, a survey made in 1855 (when Ireland was struggling to recover from the trauma of the Great Famine) shows the pattern of land ownership in the country then. I happen to have the list of

172

landowners owning 2,000 acres or more for County Clare, the county to the south of Connemara and just as poor. The Marquis Thomond owned a nice little parcel of just 24,700 acres, Colonel George Wyndham just 23,700, Nicholas Westby 15,400, Marquis Conyngham had to do with a measly 14,100 acres — but why go on? There were forty-three people in all owning 2,000 acres or more in that county.

As for the tenants — the people who actually did the farming and grew the food — 16,000 of the farmers in County Clare, according to the Valuation, farmed less than four acres; another 16,000 held no land at all, but worked as labourers for farmers who were themselves on the verge of starvation. Here perhaps I may be allowed to quote once more from the writings of that sturdy English yeoman, William Cobbet. In a letter to his Political Journal, written while on his travels in Ireland, he writes of the very fertile county of Kilkenny:

'The farmer and his family are all in half nakedness ... They raise wheat and oats and barley and butter and pork in great abundance; but never do they *taste* any of either, except perchance a small part of the meal of the oats. Potatoes are their sole food.'

And, of the tens of thousands of destitute country people who had fled to Dublin to beg for food, he wrote:

'I saw Turvill's pigstye the day before I came off, and I solemnly declare, in the face of England and of Ireland, that Turvill's two hogs were better lodged, and far better fed, and far more clean in their skins, than are thousands and thousands of the human beings in this city; which, as to streets, squares, and buildings, is as fine a city as almost anywhere in the world.'

Not surprisingly did desperate tenants band themselves into secret societies, such as the Terry Alts, a band that was particularly active around County Clare. There were plenty of these societies all over the country, and their activities gave rise to what became known as 'agrarian outrages'. The government, and the police of course, took a lively interest in these, and figures were published every year detailing the number of incidents and casualties. In 1881 there were 1,235 agrarian outrages reported by the police in Connaught alone (there were 4,439 in Ireland as a whole), of which nine involved homicide.

But in that same year there were 767 evictions in Connaught (a total of 3,221 in all of Ireland). Evictions were carried out when tenants couldn't pay their rent, and are very much part of the folk memory of Irish country people; there are ballads and poems about them, paintings, and also many photographs. The elements are always the same: armed police, often soldiers as well; a battering ram to smash down the door; thin women clutching babies to their breasts; old people being carried out in chairs or hobbling out on crutches; very often the thatch being dragged off the roof, the stones of the house split assunder with crowbars, and sometimes the whole place set on fire.

The 'outrages' were very much the result of the evictions. The eviction procedure had to be preceded by 'process serving', and because the letter from the magistrate actually had to be handed to the defaulting tenant, the process servers tended to have a rather bad time of it at the hands of the tenants' societies. Eventually it was necessary always to provide them with an armed escort. When land previously farmed by the evicted tenants was offered for rent to other people, the Terry Alts and their like would ward of anyone thinking of taking over such tenancies with threats. Landlords' agents who were too rapacious were threatened too, and a few of them actually lost their lives.

Why I am such an admirer of Michael Davitt is that he, alone I believe of all Irish nationalist politicians, realized that the question of land ownership was the most important question of all. It doesn't matter much, really, who rules a country — what matters is who owns it. John Devoy, a member of the Fenian brotherhood in America, summed up the whole matter of Ireland's problems in 1878:

'I think the only true solution of the land question is the abolition of landlordism. The landlord system is the greatest curse inflicted by England on Ireland, and Ireland will never be prosperous or happy until it is rooted out. The land of Ireland belongs to the people of Ireland and to them alone, and we must not be afraid to say so.'

Davitt was not afraid to say so. Born in 1846 on a small tenant farm in County Mayo, he had first-hand experience of the injustices of the system. His parents were still reeling from the famine (they were lucky to have survived it) when they found themselves unable to pay their rent.

Eviction followed and the family — mother, father and four children — were thrown out on the road and their house burned.

There was nothing at all unusual in this. All during the years of the Great Famine (during which one million people died in excess of the normal death-rate) evictions went on at a furious pace. The landlords simply wanted to get rid of their tenants at any price, so that they could amalgamate the holdings into large farms, and let these to men with capital for far higher rents. Even as early as 1838, before the famine, Colonel Wyndham (he who in 1855 owned 23,700 acres) made, to those of his tenants who were not doing well: 'an opportunity of emigrating to Canada, at considerable expence to myself. There is plenty of good land there entirely unoccupied, and very many of your countrymen are realizing property there every day. The tenantry are informed that they will have from this time until next March to consider duly the proposal of emigration. All will pay their rent as hitherto until next March.' But of course, not everybody wanted to emigrate to Canada, and as the famine years rolled on and people could not pay their rents eviction was the answer.

What a choice: eviction or emigration if you were lucky, starvation if you weren't. Throughout all this suffering the English authorities failed to stop even one person in Ireland from dying, though they were very good at counting them. After the 1851 census, Lady Wilde wrote a poem called 'The Exodus':

> 'A million a decade! Calmly and cold
> The units are read by our statesmen sage;
> Little they think of a Nation old,
> Fading away from history's page;
> Outcast leaves by a desolate sea —
> Fallen leaves of humanity.
>
> 'A million a decade!' — of human wrecks,
> Corpses lying in fever sheds —
> Corpses huddled on foundering decks,
> And shroudless dead on their rocky beds;
> Nerve and muscle and heart and brain,
> Lost to Ireland — lost in vain.

After lamenting the fact that this million people died without advancing the

cause of Ireland's freedom one jot, she goes on to address the enormously
wealthy aristocracy that ran the government, and stood by and watched the
people die:

> Was it for this you plighted your word,
> Crowned and crownless rulers of men?
> Have you kept faith with your crucified Lord,
> And fed his sheep till He comes again?
> Or fled like hireling shepherds away,
> Leaving the sheep to the gaunt wolf's prey?
>
> Have ye given of your purple to cover,
> Have ye given of your gold to cheer,
> Have ye given of your love, as a lover
> Might cherish the bride he held dear,
> Broken the Sacrament-bread to feed
> Souls and bodies in uttermost need?
>
> Ye stand at the Judgement-bar today —
> The Angels are counting the dead-roll too;
> Have ye trod in the pure and perfect way,
> And ruled for God as the crowned should do?
> Count our dead — before Angels and men,
> Ye're judged and doomed by the statist's pen.

When Angela and I used to return to our little caravan in the evenings,
after wandering through the rocks of Connemara, happening on yet another
dead hamlet in the hills with little piles of stones showing where homes had
been, and slightly ridged ground indicating the lazy beds of old, now tumbled
back to grass, we felt compelled to read our books of Irish history. I found
it difficult — and still do — to read about the Great Famine (there were
many other famines of course, but it is the potato famine of 1845 that all
the books are about) because such a state of fury and sadness comes over
me that I cannot go on. Every history of Ireland that I have so far read is
full of eyewitness accounts of the effects of the famine which are too deeply
disturbing, too harrowing. I stepped over the dead and dying bodies that
littered the street of Chowringhee (Calcutta's posh thoroughfare) during the
great Bengal famine of 1942–3, and in Ireland, too, many of the men crawled

out of their cabins to die outside, in the fields, because they could not bear to lie and watch the death agonies of their wives and little children, and the rats gnawing at their bodies.

I do not blame the English — there were starving people in England too, and the Scottish lairds were at that very time calling in the troops to evict the crofters from their cabins before burning them down, in the Highland Clearances. I blame the landlord system that allows one man to own the land of others and extract vast amounts of unearned rent from it. It is easy to blame the potato blight, yet if the farmers of Ireland had been allowed to keep the fruits of their farming in the years before the famine they would have had enough reserves to last them through the blight years. Even more dammingly, government figures and the annual reports of port authorities record that during every year of the famine huge amounts of wheat, barley, meat, butter and other agricultural produce were being exported to England. The British parliament at that time was totally committed to the philosophy of *laissez-faire*, and 'political economy', so whenever an Irish member suggested that the export of food from a starving country should be temporarily stopped he was opposed on the grounds that 'it would interfere with the free workings of the market.'

Eventually, the prime minister, Robert Peel, relented so far as to obtain some shipments of 'Indian corn' (maize) from the United States. That, apparently, was all right because it was not a normal article of commerce in Britain and so its distribution would not interfere with the sacred workings of the market. But it was not to be given to the starving people. It was to be sold to them, for money, which of course they did not have. Public works were started all over Ireland (chiefly constructing unnecessary roads, and harbours into which no ship could get) so that they could earn the money they needed. The fact that the starving people were so weak they could not even crawl to work was not taken into account at all. The Indian corn remained unsold and was kept locked up in warehouses closely guarded by armed soldiers.

Neither Peel, nor any of the learned historians whose books I have read, realized a simple thing: that subsistence peasants do not fit into an industrial revolution. They play no part in it; they act neither as a market for industrial goods, nor as producers of them; they are simply in the way. I remember an argument I had with the District Commissioner of Sesheke District, in Barotseland (now Western Province) of Northern Rhodesia (now Zambia) before the Second World War. His principal job was collecting poll

177

tax and hut tax from the natives. I said to him, 'What right have we got exacting cash taxes from these people? They have a subsistence economy and never handle cash.'

'They must be made to,' he said. 'They must be driven into the cash economy. To pay the taxes, the young men have to go to the Cooperbelt and work in the mines; the old men have to rear a surplus of cattle, which they sell for cash, to feed the people in the towns along the railway line, and a surplus of maize too. They must be forced into a cash economy. As it is, they are doing no good to anybody — they might as well not exist.'

'They might as well not exist'! Presumably that is how the rulers of industrialized Britain thought of the Irish subsistence farmers. In the mid-eighteenth century, Britain and Ireland were in the full throes of an almost violent industrial revolution. Anything that stood in the way of it was to be swept out of the way. There is a most revealing passage from *The Times*, (quoted in *The Story of the Irish Race* by Seamus MacManus) which sees the real position quite clearly:

They are going! They are going! The Irish are going with a vengeance. Soon a Celt will be as rare in Ireland as a Red Indian on the shores of Manhattan. Law has ridden through Ireland: it has been taught with bayonets, and interpreted with ruin. Townships levelled with the ground, straggling columns of exiles, workhouses multiplied and still crowded, express the determination of the legislature to rescue Ireland from its slovenly old barbarism, and to plant there the institutions of this more civilized land.'

The ancestor of a neighbouring family that lives just down the road from me, Sir Arthur Chichester, had voiced similar sentiments in 1602, after the rebellion of the O'Neills and the O'Donnells had been put down by a scorched earth policy:

'No course will cut the throat of the grand traitors, subject limbs and bring the country into quiet, but famine, which is well begun and will daily increase.

When they are down, it must be good laws, severe punishment, abolishing their ceremonies and customs, and lordlike Irish government, keeping them without arms . . . that must bridle them and keep them in perpetual obedience.'

178

But *The Times*'s leader-writer was to be disappointed. Although the population of Ireland dropped from 8,175,124 in 1841 to 6,552,386 in 1851, still some Celts survived, unlike the Red Indians in Manhattan. And this is another reason why I am interested in Michael Davitt, because I think it was he, more than any other one man, who saved what was left of them.

Angela and I were motoring up through County Mayo one day when Angela suddenly called, 'Stop! Stop!'

'What's the matter?' I asked.

'Look, this is Straide.'

'What of it?'

'Michael Davitt! It's where Michael Davitt was born!'

We had come to a tiny scattering of houses, where there had once been a populous village (Davitt writes in his memoirs how three hundred women, men and children, or at least their dead bodies, had been flung into one pit in the workhouse yard at nearby Swinford). There was the usual desecrated Franciscan friary, which we looked at. I asked a council worker who was tidying up there if Davitt was buried nearby. He took us to his grave, and personally I got a much greater buzz from it than I ever got standing by the tomb of Nelson, or Wellington, or any other illustrious cadaver.

Nearby we found the Michael Davitt National Memorial Museum, and in it many photographs taken of, and by, Davitt, and much memorabilia. We had both already read that masterly biography, *Davitt and Irish Revolution 1846–82*, by T. W. Moody, so were well acquainted with his life story. The Davitts, after they were evicted from their home when Michael was four, managed to get to Lancashire where they all got work in a cotton mill. Michael started work in it when he was nine, earning just two shillings and sixpence for a sixty-hour week. Two years later he had his right arm mangled in a machine and had to have it amputated just below the shoulder. This, though a personal tragedy for him, was good for Ireland because it freed him to be educated.

He joined the Irish Republican Brotherhood, the object of which was to free Ireland by force from English domination. Of course it did not succeed (a tiny disunited nation cannot hope to overcome the greatest military power in the world) and Davitt got imprisoned for gun-running. He served seven years, mostly in Dartmoor, where no doubt he managed to receive some more education, of a sort.

On being released, as the result of an amnesty, he returned to Ireland

and found himself a hero. His family had by then emigrated to America, and when he went there to see them John Devoy, the great American Fenian, organized a lecture tour for him. He consequently toured the States, and was a tremendous success in arousing sympathy for Ireland among the millions of Irish among the population.

When he returned to Ireland he toured his old county of Mayo, and found the most grinding poverty there, rack-renting in full swing, and violent evictions commonplace. At Irishtown, in County Mayo, an absentee landlord, named Bourke, had instructed his agent to carry out more evictions on his estate, and in April 1879 the enraged tenants, together with thousands of supporters, called a meeting. Davitt was asked to organize it, and did so, and it was there that the idea of the Land League was born.

This meeting changed Davitt's life. He might have just gone on being an urban Fenian intellectual, helping to carry on a completely ineffectual campaign against the government, completely out of touch with the only people who really mattered: the farmers. Instead he decided to join his strength unreservedly with the latter, and at another meeting (on 16 August 1879, in Daly's Hotel, Castlebar, now the Imperial) the Land League was formally born.

Davitt's strength was that he was a true Gandhian, before Gandhi was born; he invented the principle of passive resistance, of non-violence. All over Ireland the farmers joined the Land League; they contributed a few pennies a month to a fund to help evicted tenants; they took vows promising never to take up land from which another tenant had been evicted; they started rent strikes against unfair rents; and they made full use of the boycott, the social isolation of and economic non-cooperation with landlords or their agents who were too rapacious. Davitt travelled indefatigably, holding meetings. He once addressed a huge crowd from a platform erected over the foundations of his old home, where he said, 'If I am standing upon a platform erected over the ruins of my levelled home, I may yet have the satisfaction of trampling on the ruins of Irish landlordism.'

Well, he did. The authorities put him in jail from time to time, as they did Parnell, whom Davitt co-opted to help lead the Land League. They outlawed the League (the Ladies' Land League had already been set up to take over the League's work — they then had to outlaw that too). They passed 'coercion laws' one after another, giving the police the right of summary arrest, imprisonment without trial and all the rest of it. They flooded Ireland with soldiers. But they could not put out the fire. At last, for

180

the first time, the real people of the Irish countryside were involved, not just a parcel of city-bred intellectuals, and the Raj in Ireland was doomed. Gladstone was forced to pass act after act in the English parliament to provide tenants with the money to purchase their land from their landlords, who were now only too delighted to sell because they could no longer collect the rents. In one generation, the land of Ireland passed into the ownership of the Irish people. The English ruling class had no more effective business there and mostly withdrew, or started to engage in honest trade. Many Irish patriots are honoured far more than Davitt, but I am convinced that he did more than any others, martyred or not, to make his country free.

Now, my neighbours — my neighbours here where I live and write this — have freedom and independence, owning their own farms, working hard to make a fair living, and never having to bow their heads to anybody at all, except at Mass every Sunday at Ballykelly church. But it was a long time coming:

> One by one they're falling round us, their pale faces to the sky;
> We've no strength to dig them graves — there let them lie.
> The wild bird, if he's stricken, is mourned by the others,
> But we — we die in Christian land, — we die amid our brothers,
> In a land that God has given us, like a wild beast in his cave,
> Without a tear, a prayer, a shroud, a coffin or a grave.
> Ha! but think ye the contortions on each livid face ye see,
> Will not be read on Judgement-day by eyes of Deity?

from *The Famine Year*, by Lady Wilde.

CHAPTER TWENTY

~

In Search of
Father McDyer

I WANTED TO GO ON UP to the far north-west corner of Ireland, to County Donegal. I wanted to go there to meet old friends; for way back in 1960, or thereabouts, I had gone to that far-flung corner of Europe looking for a man named Father McDyer. Strange rumours had reached me, on my farm in Pembrokeshire in West Wales, of some wonderful man, parish priest of the wildest, coldest, wettest, windiest and most remote parish in Ireland, who had managed to stem the emigration from his area by teaching his flock how to survive and make a living there. I was making a living at that time by farming some sixty-odd acres of wet woodland, swamp, rocks and sour land in Pembrokeshire; I was witnessing the exodus of my old Welsh-speaking neighbours, or at least of their children, and their replacement by yuppy holidaymakers from England; and I thought I could learn something that might be of use. So, calling on my old allies at the BBC, and another old ally (and respected friend), Michael Huxley, the Editor of the *Geographical Magazine*, to finance me, I set out with notebook and tape recorder to furthest Donegal to hunt for the mysterious priest.

I drove to Killybegs, which is in a sheltered bay on the south coast of the Donegal peninsular, and the most important fishing port on the west coast of Ireland. It was like a gold-rush town. The Irish fishermen had only recently discovered modern fishing trawlers, and here was a great fleet of them, mostly old French or Belgian ships, thumping in from the sea. Their holds were crammed with herring which they had taken with their huge purse-seine nets, and these were being pumped into a factory to be ground up into fish meal for battery hens, broiler-house chickens, and pigs. I noticed that large new bungalows had recently sprung up near the town,

182

the latest thing in Texan ranch-house architecture, and there were plenty of large modern cars about. I went into a pub and tough-looking men in blue jerseys were shoving money across the bar with great abandon, and whiskey and stout were coming the other way.

A short, stocky, middle-aged skipper had a few drinks with me and said that, what with generous government loans to buy new boats and the fish-meal factory with its ever-open maw, the fishermen of Killybegs had never had it so good. 'But ye can't go on mowing the grass for ever and expect cattle to fatten on the pasture,' he said. Another fisherman agreed with him, but said, 'Anyway, we're making plenty of money while it lasts.'

I went for a walk around the harbour, and came across a small German freighter. Eight hundred tons of coal were being shovelled out of her holds by a dozen hard-looking farmers wielding hand-shovels. They threw the coal into big steel containers which were then hoisted ashore by a crane. Have they never heard of grabs, I thought. But then, no doubt the few shillings they would be earning were welcome to them, and they looked to be enjoying the work.

I continued westward, and cannot tell you how lovely the countryside was about there. The sea rolled far below me on my left hand, and far away over it I could just see the mountains of Sligo, looking like a different land; the coast was indented with bays and headlands. To my right rose green mountains, their lower slopes dotted with whitewashed houses, many of them with thatched roofs. Near each house were some small conical stacks of hay, often some of oats, and long, tall piles of turf, or peat, already dried for the winter fire. When you came into the lee of a house, the pleasant, pungent smell of burning peat hit your nostrils. I felt a great air of peace and happiness about this countryside, and I couldn't help feeling that it was sad that so many of these people left and went elsewhere. (I thought of Camden Town, and Kilburn, and gave a little shudder.)

I cut inland to avoid the mighty split mountain of Slieve League, split by the sea itself, though I afterwards did climb up it, in such a blinding rainstorm that when I got to the top I nearly fell over the edge and down that mighty cliff. I passed a little bungalow, modern and tile-roofed, I heard the unmistakeable sound of a loom. I knocked on the door, and found a young man working at a flying-shuttle hand loom.

He stopped and told me his name was Michael Byrne. He was weaving the Donegal tweed which was as famous in those days, and as good, as Harris tweed from the Hebrides. He told me he earned about eight pounds a week if he stuck at it, and still had time to run his little smallholding, for he only had to work five hours a day at his weaving. I must explain that eight pounds then was worth about eighty pounds today: not enough for a family to live on in any style but enough to get by on nevertheless. Seeing that my friend also had a couple of cows, a pig or two, a fishing boat, a potato patch, and some turf to dig, I would say that, though not exactly 'ridin' high on the hog' as my American cousins would put it, he was OK.

But he told me that the comparative affluence of the Donegal hand weavers was quite a new thing. His father, he said, had worked for a private firm in Donegal town, which supplied the webs (the warps, which are the longitudinal threads of a piece of cloth) and paid for the completed length of cloth. He had had to work at his loom from seven in the morning to nine at night to weave two webs a week, and for each web he got three pounds. Admittedly at that time six pounds a week was not a bad wage for, say, a labourer, but weaving is a skilled job and besides, nobody should have to work fourteen hours a day at anything.

'Why is it so much better now?' I asked.

'Oh, Father McDyer — the Father has changed everything.'

'How?'

'Why, we have our own co-operative now, the hand weavers' co-operative. We run our own warping mill, which makes our warps for us, and McDyer has fixed up marketing arrangements for us in New York. We get a fair price for our work now. Before, the Donegal firm made all the profit.'

Leaving him to his weaving, I walked on westward again, over unpeopled and mountainous country, until I came to a small thatched cabin, with the usual tiny hay stacks, oat stack, peat stack, and sizeable garden. I looked at the garden and saw that most of it was planted with celery. Well, I had heard of the Irish living on potatoes but never on celery, and when a man came round the corner of the house I asked him what he grew it for.

'Oh, Father McDyer,' he said, 'it's all his doing. It's a co-operative ye see. He's after gettin' us all to grow celery. It goes to the co-op factory and we gets paid for it.'

'Do you make much out of it?'

'Oh, it's worth it, it's worth it: few pounds more'n we got before. There's many of us would have given up and gone to England if it hadn't been for the celery. And, mind, I have a daughter who works in the canning factory that cans it and she brings back a few pounds too. It all helps, it all helps.'

The road took me into a steep-sided valley, with rather barren mountain-side rising up on my left and the floor of the valley far down on my right. On the opposite slope of the valley, which was south-facing, was a scattering of houses, perhaps half of them thatched, the rest tiled, and there were clearings and improved land near the houses: good grassland for the sheep when they came down from the mountain for lambing, and gardens dug up into lazy beds for potatoes. Eventually I got a glimpse of the sea before me — the valley wound steeply down to it — and I could see a church and the signs of a village. This, I realized, was Glencolumkille.

I speeded up my steps, which had been lagging a bit (I had been wondering if I had not been foolish to leave my car behind in Killybegs after all, but when I got a sight of my goal I was glad I had), and I swung down the narrow deserted road towards the village. Yes, thank God, there was a pub, and thank Him even more warmly it was open. I shot into it like a ferret down a rabbit hole. Inside was a group of fishermen, or fishermen-farmers I suppose they were, talking over their Guinness. I joined them. And lo and behold they were talking about the man I was looking for. I gathered from listening to their conversation that McDyer had been after starting a fishermen's co-operative.

'We were all against it,' said one. 'Held out right against it. We didn't want to be told what to do, who to sell our fish to.'

I asked them what had made them change their minds, and they told me the following story.

'We went out one Sunday morning and had such a powerful draught of fish — herring — it nearly sunk the boat.'

On coming ashore, they came up to the pub and telephoned the fish-meal factory at Killybegs. The caretaker there told them that no lorry could be sent for the fish until Wednesday at the earliest, and that in any case the factory was glutted with herring from the big ring-netters.

'All those fish and we had no sale for them. So we were having a few drinks, "waking" the fish. We knew we'd got to fling 'em back in the sea.' (Waking meant holding a wake over them, a funeral celebration.)

And in walked Father McDyer. They told him their sad story; they were very hard up, and they hoped the Father might find them the price of a pint each.

'How much are you asking for the fish?' asked the Father.

They told him how much they would have got from the fish-meal factory, which of course was a very low price.

'All right, here's the money,' said McDyer, and he counted the cash out on to the bar.

McDyer walked over to see one of his parishioners who owned a small truck, which he managed to hire for a small fee as the man had no work for it on a Sunday. He picked up a couple of his altar boys to help him, drove down to the little harbour, and loaded the herring. He then drove up into the mountains.

Now Irish country people, even if they live just a mile or two from the sea, do not have much of a tradition of eating fish, but they do love herring. Sometimes, my fishermen friends down at Duncannon or Ballyhack will fling a spare box of herring into the boot of my car, other times I haggle with them to buy a box and get hundreds of fine fat herring for under a fiver. We salt some, freeze some, eat them fresh until we are stuffed with them, and then dole out the surplus to our farmer neighbours. They love them. White fish they do not seem to be so fond of — it would never occur to them to buy any — but herring, yes, they know all about herring. So Father McDyer drove through the mountains, for the whole of the livelong day, and knocked on every lonely farmhouse door that he came to; and he sold all the herring, at a very good price.

'He came back into this pub,' said one of the fishermen, 'and we were still here spending some of the money your man gave us for the fish. Well, he came in and emptied a damn great bag of cash out on to the bar. A huge heap it was, a powerful heap of money. We thought the good man was going to share it out between us all, but not on yer life. He stood us all a drink, that was all, then he made us a speech.'

The speech, I gathered, urged them to buck their ideas up: 'You could have done what I did. Why don't you form a fishing co-operative like I've been urging you to, buy a truck and do your own marketing?' Shamed into it, they did.

Fortified by beer and this story, which pleased me greatly, I walked over to the presbytery to try to see the great man himself. I had first to penetrate the defences put up by his housekeeper, a formidable lady who guarded what little privacy he had with iron determination: the Father was out, the Father was eating, the Father was resting, the Father was not to be disturbed.

However, determination won, and, next day, I was admitted into the study of the great man. I took to him unreservedly and he seemed to feel that I was worth spending time with too. I spent a week at Glencolumkille, putting up in a B and B and being driven around by Father McDyer every day to see the different activities he had established. Luckily, although McDyer has long since passed away, I an able to relate his exact words to me because I recorded them on my tape recorder and still have the tape. He had a fine, rolling, rather harsh Northern Irish accent.

'Our first objective,' he said, 'was to make the best possible use of the small amount of arable land that we have got here. It might shock you to realize that the average farm here is only about ten acres, and of that not more than two and a half or three would be arable or tillable. Consequently the first emphasis was to make the best profit or return from those little arable patches.'

So what the Father did was to form a vegetable co-operative. All who joined it agreed to grow celery in the summer, and cabbages in the winter, and a factory was set up to can the celery (it all went off to America) and dry the cabbages. A nursery was also set up, owned by the co-operative, to supply celery and cabbage plants. The whole thing was working well, and the year before I was there the co-operative paid out £8,000 to its sixty members. This may not sound much, but it was £8,000 that they did not have before, and as McDyer said, 'If the farmers achieved more expertise, then instead of that £8,000 we should be paying out about £12,000 to them for the same acreage.'

He introduced me to several farmers, who all had their small acreage of celery — maybe a quarter to half an acre — and professed themselves delighted with the scheme. We went to the canning factory, where a small army of young girls were happily working, earning a wage for themselves which had not been available before.

Then there was the weavers' co-operative, which I had already learnt about from Michael Byrne. But not only did McDyer organize the cottage weavers working from home, he also raised the money to build a big weaving shed fitted out with many looms, to be operated by the whole community. Then there was the knitters' co-operative. There is a great tradition of knitting Aran sweaters in Donegal (so called because they often incorporate Aran island motifs in their decoration). When McDyer came to the parish, sharp-eyed traders used to come round the farmhouses and villages and buy these up for as little as a pound or thirty shillings each, before selling them at astronomical prices. McDyer promptly formed a co-operative and paid the ladies £5 each for them, which made a staggering difference to their standard of living. There was also a knitting factory. This was not a co-operative, it was privately run, started by a Dublin businessman, but Father McDyer had lured him into the area. Then there was the builders' co-operative. So many people were being attracted to the now-prosperous area that it was necessary to build new houses. McDyer attracted some young builders back from Dublin and they set up a co-operative. When I was there they were busy building some traditional thatched-roof cabins which were to be let to holidaymakers, for Father McDyer had decided to try to start a tourist industry in the area.

The thing that impressed me most about the good priest's enterprises was that they were first and foremost trying to use local materials, they were non-polluting industries, and they needed very little outside finance (although a little pump-priming money from central government did not come amiss). McDyer was very anxious to start a wool processing plant and a spinning mill. Raw wool was one of the chief products of the area, and it seemed wrong to him that it should all be sent away to Bradford in England when expensive yarn had to be bought in for the knitters and weavers. As he explained into my tape recorder:

'Our whole attitude here is that our resources are meagre and our aim is to exploit to the fullest any resources that we have, whether it's in traditional crafts, or whether it's in vegetables, what you like, tourism; to exploit every possible resource; to attract as many streams of income to the family purse as possible.'

I asked him what his own motives were in going to all this trouble. I felt that I had touched a nerve somewhere, for he came back at me with some spirit, in his gravelly Northern Ireland brogue:

'Well, I'm glad you asked that question because there are several reasons motivating me myself personally. First of all I spent ten years of my life in England, which I liked very well; but one of the impressions that I got was that there were far too many young Irish people required by economic necessity in our country here to go to England. I felt that that was a slur on our country, that we should have to depend on another country to absorb so much of our youth. Consequently when I came home I was determined that the first parish I was assigned to I would do everything in my power to stem the flow of emigrants to England, or any other country. That was one reason, one motivation. Another was that the Glencolumkilles of this world, even though they are flung far and wide in the most remote places, they have something to offer which the city dweller is not aware of. And it is this: it is tranquillity; it is peace; it is lack of noise; it is living close to Nature and absorbing much fresh air; it is health; it is joy and freedom for children. And consequently I felt that if we stand back and allow the Glencolumkilles of this world to die out and become economic failures it would be a tragedy for the people of these beautiful country districts to be dispersed among the cities of this world. I felt that a stand must be made in Glencolumkille to demonstrate that even in a remote rural area people can be made viable and a community can be made prosperous.

'I am swimming against the tide, and I quite agree that the modern trend seems to be towards urbanization, towards moving towards some huge industrial combine, and that this trend will go on unless it is resisted. But it will be a tragedy if it is not resisted. I don't think it was ever intended by God or by Nature that we should all become city dwellers. I don't think it was intended by God or by Nature that we should become cogs, that we should become serfs. And I do believe strongly that the small men of this world have only one hope of resisting the new feudalism of belonging to huge industries, and that one hope rests solely in small men co-operating and making big men out of themselves. A hundred voices speaking in unison are much stronger than one thin voice speaking by itself.'

It was Angela who, the other day, typed out the above words, patiently listening to the tape with Father McDyer's voice on it, and she wrote the following words of her own under the transcription:

'If only every parish in Ireland had its Father McDyer, what a holy, healthy and happy country this would be. And to think that he was thwarted all his life by the Church hierarchy and that he should die a premature death of cancer, it makes me weep.'

And it is quite true that he was so thwarted. He had to get permission from his bishop every time he wanted to go and speak in any parish other than his own, and the difficulties put in his way were considerable. It was as though the Church was jealous of him: Why should one parish priest stand out above the others? Why should a priest concern himself with temporal things like the price of knitted jumpers? But McDyer said to me: 'I am not contented to preach to people with hungry bellies.'

The Irish government, too, did not support him as they should have done. Of course he was disturbing the *status quo* somewhat: the sharks who used to drive about the country buying jerseys for one pound and selling them on for five pounds could not have liked him much, nor the firm in Donegal town that was so happily exploiting the hand weavers; inevitably he made enemies. But he did, during his lifetime, stem the exodus from one small part of Ireland, and he gave inspiration and encouragement to many people the world over, including me. I only ever disagreed with him strongly over one matter during all the time I knew him. He was trying hard, unsuccessfully as it turned out, to persuade the farmers who had grazing rights on a certain mountain to form a co-operative, and fence the common grazing into individual holdings. I opposed this because I knew that there is nothing like sharing common grazing to encourage a sense of togetherness in a community. I used to love to go up on to Dinas Mountain in Wales once a year with my neighbours and help them round up the wild ponies, identify them, catch them and brand them, and pull some out to be sent off to Llanybyther market. It was a joint effort, where we all worked together; it was a laugh and some fun; and we all had to stay good friends. To have subdivided that mountain, so that each man had his own patch, would have destroyed all this camaraderie. We had quite a lively argument about this, but it did not dent my respect for the man.

In 1990, on my tour of Ireland with Angela, we decided to make a motorized dash up to Donegal from our caravan site at Spiddal, so that I could seek out Father McDyer, if he was still alive, and pay him my respects. We set out north from Galway city, and drove to Sligo, where there is a Lyon's Corner House café preserved intact like a fly in amber, and then on through Yeats's country again. When we finally got to Donegal Bay, in the evening, we thought we had never seen anything so beautiful. The setting sun shone its rays on the Donegal mountains, far over to the north of the bay, and they looked sublime.

We spent the night in Donegal town, and set out westward next morning to Glencolumkille. Yes, Michael Byrne was still there. He lives in quite a large modern bungalow now. His loom is still set up, and it has a warp on it, but I believe it is seldom used. Instead, Michael sells Aran sweaters, and runs quite a profitable-looking shop. He is obviously doing all right, but I rather gathered from talking to him that the hand-weaving industry is in almost terminal decline.

Father McDyer, he told us, was unfortunately dead; and the celery canning factory had been converted into a fish processing factory, freeze-drying herring roes, crabs, and other fish for the Japanese market. Many of the other enterprises started by Father McDyer had changed over the years, too, but his influence can still be strongly seen and felt. Everyone we met spoke most highly of him. In Glencolumkille we found a lady named Christina Daly, in what has come to be known as the Folk Village. There is a museum there now and she is partly responsible for it. She told us that her father had moved, with all his family, to Glencolumkille because he had so admired what McDyer was doing. She had lived there ever since; she loved the place, and it was obvious she revered the memory of McDyer. She, too, felt that he had not been supported enough by either Church or state.

But maybe all true progress is made by those who reject and are rejected by the establishment, stubborn individuals who will take on the impossible and not take no for an answer. They will always at least partly fail, but sow some seeds which will, perhaps, germinate after they have gone and grow into something great and beautiful. Perhaps, when our present socio-economic system begins to falter, the example set by people such as Father McDyer will be of inspiration and strength. Perhaps some of the men and women who left the beautiful but poor country places of Ireland to go and live in the ghettos of foreign cities will come back again and really strive to make the small local economic communities work, content with good, satisfying, and simple lives, and living on Adam's cheer again. When they do, I hope some of them will remember the name of Father McDyer, for it deserves to be remembered.

As for Angela and me, we strolled down to the little harbour on that furthest promontory jutting out bravely into the wild Atlantic. We found a brace of heavy clinker-built boats drawn up on the slip; the stone steps down to the water were littered with crab shells. There were salmon and herring drift nets up on the quay, and a stack of lobster pots; but no people. It was perfectly quiet and still.

There is an ancient legend in Ireland of a land which appears every seven years above the sea towards the west. They call it *Hy-Brasail*. If you can get there, it is said, you will live for ever in great contentment, for it is the land of youth, plenty and happiness. I thought of this as we stood on the quay, gazing over the ocean. I strained my eyes, and could half imagine that I saw faint mountains just like the ones that I had seen from the top of Carn Ingli, near my farm in Pembrokeshire. But I could not. I saw no mountains. And then I thought: well, maybe I am already there, I have already found it — *Hy-Brasail* — the Blessed Isle.

～